T0367428

NOW

& NOW

Transformational Diaries of
Present Moment Living

ROB GINNIVAN

BALBOA.
PRESS

A DIVISION OF HAY HOUSE

Copyright © 2016 Rob Ginnivan.

All rights reserved. No part of this book may be used or reproduced by any means, graphic, electronic, or mechanical, including photocopying, recording, taping or by any information storage retrieval system without the written permission of the author except in the case of brief quotations embodied in critical articles and reviews.

Balboa Press books may be ordered through booksellers or by contacting:

Balboa Press
A Division of Hay House
1663 Liberty Drive
Bloomington, IN 47403
www.balboapress.com
1 (877) 407-4847

Because of the dynamic nature of the Internet, any web addresses or links contained in this book may have changed since publication and may no longer be valid. The views expressed in this work are solely those of the author and do not necessarily reflect the views of the publisher, and the publisher hereby disclaims any responsibility for them.

The author of this book does not dispense medical advice or prescribe the use of any technique as a form of treatment for physical, emotional, or medical problems without the advice of a physician, either directly or indirectly. The intent of the author is only to offer information of a general nature to help you in your quest for emotional and spiritual well-being. In the event you use any of the information in this book for yourself, which is your constitutional right, the author and the publisher assume no responsibility for your actions.

Any people depicted in stock imagery provided by Thinkstock are models, and such images are being used for illustrative purposes only. Certain stock imagery © Thinkstock.

Print information available on the last page.

ISBN: 978-1-5043-0173-2 (sc)
ISBN: 978-1-5043-0174-9 (e)

Balboa Press rev. date: 04/06/2016

CONTENTS

Acknowledgments vii
Prologue..ix
Present Moment Living ix

Chapter 1   Eating.. 1
Chapter 2   Working 16
Chapter 3   Loving.. 31
Chapter 4   Giving..45
Chapter 5   Creating...59
Chapter 6   Driving 73
Chapter 7   Exercising...86
Chapter 8   Sleeping & Dreaming 100
Chapter 9   Feeling 114
Chapter 10 Playing & Laughing 127
Chapter 11 Travelling 141
Chapter 12 Vacationing..154
Chapter 13 Knowing & Being.................................. 169
Chapter 14 Connecting 184
Chapter 15 Wondering...200
Chapter 16 Meditating & Awakening.................... 213
Chapter 17 Their Healing 228

Epilogue 241

ACKNOWLEDGMENTS

With heartfelt gratitude, I acknowledge Deepak Chopra, Eckhart Tolle and Baron Baptiste for personally helping me to shift consciousness and become awakened to infinite possibilities. Bryony Sutherland, Leon Nacson, Diana Timmins and George Yacoub then appeared on the path of synchronicity that has made the birth of Now & Now enter the world in style. And thank you to my lovely children Jesper, Annika and Oscar for teaching me what it's like living in the present moment.

PRESENT MOMENT LIVING

At the ripe young age of thirty-four, I was responsible for a large portfolio in the Information Technology industry. Buckling beneath the pressure, I was overweight, burnt out, stressed out, and suffering from anxiety; frequently turning to excessive alcohol and processed fatty food for comfort. There seemed no way out of this rut, until one pivotal day when my doctor gave me some vital home truths: my lifestyle was heading down a path to destruction.

On the way home from this particular consultation, an awakening occurred. Noticeably short of breath, I stopped the car on the side of the road. Sitting still, I closed my eyes and began consciously controlling my breathing. A deep sense of calm and peace overcame me, which was ultimately the catalyst for the development of my meditation and mindfulness practice. That ten-minute exercise was a pivotal moment in my life, as I hit a fork on the path and chose a healthy spiritual direction instead. From that day onwards, I actively pursued 'Present Moment Living' and quickly concluded that being controlled by thoughts of the past and worries about the future is not the means to attaining joy, happiness and peace. No matter how clouded we are by the busyness of the mind, the everyday stresses of life and the sometimes seemingly 'no way out', it is possible to rise above the canvas of pervasive thoughts and access our true selves – the soul. And due to my positive transformation and realisation that 'impossible is nothing', I am committed to inspire, motivate and enlighten as many people as I can with these values and techniques.

Since childhood, I have often been in positions of leadership; ranging from playing the lead role of Jesus in my elementary school's Christian Passion Play, through to school prefect, captain of various basketball teams, and management of corporate groups. After accessing higher states of consciousness through consistent meditation, I became enlightened to a compassionate way of being. Inspired by my own transformation and leadership influence from world yoga revolutionist, Baron Baptiste, I began working with contemporary war veterans suffering with Post-Traumatic Stress Disorder (PTSD) as a yoga teacher and mindfulness coach for a non-profit charity organisation bringing free services to Soldier On (a charity reintegrating serving and ex-serving men and women into the Australian community). My co-owned Canberra based business, Tidy Temple Yoga (co-founded in 2012), also became a fundraising sponsor for Lifeline's suicide prevention in 2013.

After studying the Heart Sutra and the Eight Verses of Mind Training with His Holiness, the Dalai Lama, that same year, then spending time with spiritual teachers, Deepak Chopra, M.D., and Eckhart Tolle in 2014, I put myself in a position to be of service to people all over the planet by packaging up these teachings and making them accessible to everyone willing to listen and evolve.

In 2013, I began journaling my experiences of living 'in the now'. As a result, I experienced a profound shift through varying dimensions of consciousness. One astounding example – which a neurosurgeon could only explain as a miracle – was gaining a sense of smell for the first time in my life at the age of forty-eight. Until this time I cannot recall ever smelling at all, even as a child. Doctors over the years had their theories and I was left wondering on a constant basis what it would be like to have this sense working. My first smell situation was that of a homeless person. The second smell was chilli and garlic cooking on a stovetop. It was so exciting and akin to being born again.

Another instance was the birth of a radically creative idea acquired during meditation, in which I decided to become the first person to run a half marathon (approximately 21 kilometres) in a hot-air balloon, on a treadmill powered by a generator. This 'world's first' adventure raised $5,000 for The Heart Foundation against cardiovascular disease and earned me a place in the 2013 edition of *Ripley's Believe It Or Not*.

Through my Meditation & Mindfulness practice and teachings for over sixteen years, I continue to help thousands of people to shift consciousness, and access a deeper sense of calm and enhanced focus through the power and wisdom of being in the now on a constant basis and continuum through life. My teachings and work continue to be published in a variety of journals and magazines, and now through this book. Shortly I will be embarking on a mindfulness tour – Consciousness Across

Australia – offering complimentary teaching sessions to people in many towns and cities over a period of many weeks.

Present Moment Living, also known as Mindfulness, has been practiced for thousands of years in one way or another. It is only within the last thirty-five years that it has gained popularity in the Western world with the likes of Australian-born 2009 Nobel Prize winner in Physiology or Medicine, Professor Elizabeth Blackburn. One of Blackburn's studies looked at the effects of a three-month meditation retreat on telomerase activity. Telomerase is an enzyme, discovered by Professor Blackburn and Professor Carol Greider, that is related to the ageing of cells. The study found that, "increases in perceived control and decreases in negative affectivity" contributed to an increase in telomerase activity, which implied the lengthening of telomeres and immune cell longevity.

Another leader in this field is Jon Kabat-Zinn, PhD, MIT. In 1979, Kabat-Zinn founded the Mindfulness-Based Stress Reduction (MBSR) programme at the University of Massachusetts to help treat chronically ill people. MBSR programmes are now applied all over the world in schools, veteran reintegration centres, hospitals, correctional institutions and corporations. And the 'mother of mindfulness' Ellen J Langer, Harvard professor of psychology continues to educate society by distinguishing mindlessness versus mindfulness.

Present Moment Living

Mindfulness practice means that we commit fully in each moment to be present; inviting ourselves to interface with this moment in full awareness, with the intention to embody as best we can an orientation of calmness, mindfulness, and equanimity right here and right now.

Jon Kabat-Zinn, *Wherever You Go, There You Are: Mindfulness Meditation in Everyday Life*

As you read this book, be mindful of the sensations that exist in your hands and feet. Whenever the mind lures you back into the past or far into the future, take a deep breath in and a deep breath out, smile and come back to the present moment. It is easy to be distracted before we suddenly return to the present moment and realise we have turned page after page and looked at the words, but not truly read them, and have no idea what has happened in the story! There is nothing more powerful than being in the now. By simply noticing something new is being in the present moment.

As soon as you honor the present moment, all unhappiness and struggle dissolve, and life begins to flow with joy and ease. When you act out the present-moment awareness, whatever you do becomes imbued with a sense of quality, care, and love – even the most simple action.

Eckhart Tolle, *The Power of Now: A Guide to Spiritual Enlightenment*

There is a deep calming stillness of consciousness that exists above the canvas of the busy, chattering mind. By focusing on your next three inhales/exhales, you will find a new sense of calmness enters your body and mind. Try it now.

The mind and consciousness are separate from each other – meaning that the soul is the witness and observer of thoughts. Many people, however, identify themselves with past experiences. The mind is not a fan of the present moment and likes to consume consciousness. The past does not exist anymore in reality – only in the mind. So the good news is that when we pay full attention to the present moment and what is going on within our bodies and surroundings, the past and future dissolve, at least for this moment.

There are tremendous benefits that arise from mindfulness practice, but it works precisely because we don't *try to attain benefit. Instead, we befriend ourselves as we are. We learn how to drop in on ourselves, visit, and hang out in awareness.*

<u>Jon Kabat-Zinn, TIME magazine</u>

So, right now, practice mindfulness by observing your surroundings in a non-judgemental way and without labelling anything you see. Look up at the sky or across at something in front of you, feel the texture of the book you are holding, listen to the sounds within your vicinity. Taste any food or drink if it is within reach and be mindful of smells currently existing.

Were you thinking or worrying about anything in particular during this exercise? In this day and age, there seems to be a tendency to 'overthink' unnecessarily about issues, events and situations. The mind is more seductive towards negative thoughts than positive thoughts. The temptation of reaching for a handheld device to check social media messages is distracting. Yes, of course there is a time to think and plan for continuing to function and live life. Once you have thought about it and know what you need to do, come back to the present moment and rest in a state of being.

This doesn't mean that we should live in a catatonic state or walk around like zombies. When adopting a consistent mindfulness practice, you will begin to experience a deeper level of Presence. And whilst we keep functioning with purpose – moment by moment, hour by hour, day by day – life takes on new meaning. As we evolve and continue to live in the now, amazing things occur: food tastes better, colours appear brighter, simple things and situations become more interesting, amusing and delightful. You laugh more. You feel a lightness of being, not so burdened by the past or worried about the future.

I've heard many people practicing mindfulness say that they feel a sense of peace, freedom, calm and contentment. It would be safe to say that when you are attentive to your surroundings, the mind becomes still and there is no time for distractions other than this present moment. And during this period, people experience longer gaps of being in between each thought. Over time, with regular practice, any anxious thoughts that do arise tend to not be so intense and fade away quicker than before, being evaporated by Present Moment Living.

Now, stop reading for a few seconds and simply rest in stillness. Gently close your eyes or gaze softly at the tip of your nose, and feel the Presence of a subtle energy vibrating through the legs and arms. Now, spend a few moments recounting enjoyable times gone by. The purpose of this exercise is to demonstrate that not everything from the past needs to be forgotten or suppressed. A wonderful epigram relating to this that I heard Deepak Chopra say at a retreat was along the lines of, "I use the past and don't allow the past to use me."

Mindfulness practices were originally inspired by teachings from Buddhist traditions and are now being popularised in a non-religious fashion with the assistance of scientific-based evidence. The human brain and body can benefit greatly from such methods and adaptation to lifestyle. The practice can be performed anywhere, anytime. In fact, every action taken in every waking moment can be practiced mindfully. In this day and age, the media freely promotes mindfulness in many formats, commenting on its popularity in the mainstream. Companies like Google, IBM, Nike and Facebook are leading the Mindful Revolution by introducing 'quiet rooms' in their organisations, where employees are encouraged to spend moments in contemplation. Leadership figures in these companies are themselves adopting a mindfulness practice and leading by example – that it is perfectly normal to be present, aware and compassionate to others in and out of the workplace.

In fact, it has been proven that adopting a mindfulness practice can increase productivity in less time. Annual conferences such as Wisdom 2.0 held in various locations across America and Mindful Leadership Global Forum held in Sydney, Australia, are helping shift mindfulness into the mainstream, with the attendance of employees from industry verticals such as Banking, Government, Hospitality, Manufacturing and Information Technology.

The movement has so much momentum that many believe this common sense practice will eventually be a regular part of daily life in workplaces, homes and institutions in an endeavour to bring deeper joy and happiness, inner peace, and enhanced focus and clarity.

A wonderful conduit to an effective mindfulness practice is meditation. Meditation is focusing one's mind for a period of time, in silence or with the aid of chanting. It is a practice in which an individual trains the mind or induces a mode of consciousness to simply acknowledge its content without being identified with that content.

Archaeologists and scholars agree that meditation has been around for about 5,000 years. The earliest documented records of meditation stemmed from ancient India around 3,500 years ago and it then developed in Taoist China and Buddhist India between 2,500-2,600 years ago. In 653 CE the first meditation hall opened in Japan.

Moving forward to the 18th Century, ancient translations of meditation techniques and philosophy began to travel to scholars in the West. Then in 1922, Hermann Hesse published *Siddhartha*, the story of the Buddha's spiritual journey of self-discovery. In the 1950s, the Vipassana movement (insight meditation) started in Burma. In the 1960s, Hatha Yoga and Transcendental Meditation began to gain popularity in America and Europe.

Jon Kabat-Zinn founded the Mindfulness-Based Stress Reduction program at the University of Massachusetts Medical School in 1979, which sparked the interest of mindfulness practices and meditation in the medical world. Then in 1996, Drs Deepak Chopra and David Simon founded the Chopra Center for Wellbeing. Soon after, in 1997, Eckhart Tolle published *The Power of Now: A Guide to Spiritual Enlightenment*, to introduce readers to present-moment awareness and how to tune into their deepest self. 2003 saw Deepak Chopra publish *The Spontaneous Fulfillment of Desire*, highlighting that meditation practice and a focus on our deepest desires can inspire us to turn everyday coincidences into meaningful miracles, and connect us to the field of infinite possibilities that exist in everything and anything around us.

So here we are in 2016, and you can find meditation groups, teachers, and advocates at schools, hospitals, corporate wellness initiatives, social gatherings, retreats and yoga studios all over the world in several towns and cities.

Because many people in today's society identify themselves with the past whilst placing hope in the future, they find it difficult to live in the present moment and, as a result, tend to wander around in a daydream. It becomes enlightening to understand that the only thing that really exists is this moment, *right now*. Five minutes from now does not yet exist, and five seconds ago no longer exists.

When you finally grasp this truth, a shift in consciousness occurs from the mind to a state of being. At this point a deeper sense of calm, alertness, awareness and positive energy kicks in.

We became so busy as a society over the last two decades primarily because of technological advancements and the speed at which we can now communicate. Bosses are expecting more productivity in the same amount of time. Also, generally speaking, our thirst for material possession knows no bounds. As soon as we reach one level of material comfort, we quickly become accustomed, and begin our pursuit for the next level of goodies. The catch is that this comes with more to do and more to worry about. The sudden surge and interest in mindfulness entering the mainstream is fuelled by the unprecedented levels of burnout, stress and absenteeism among individuals and organisations.

I encourage you to invest in a notebook or diary to journal your present moment experiences. As you put pen to paper, this exercise will be instrumental in assisting with your transformation through awakening and enlightening moments. And finally, as an explanation of the logo occurring throughout the book:

The circles represent thoughts that come and go on either side of the gap of 'no thought' where pure consciousness resides. The depth and understanding of a person's mindfulness practice and level of consciousness depends on the length of each 'no thought' gap in between thoughts. Many people are so overwhelmed by the process of thinking, that there is very little opportunity for the underlying peace and serenity of consciousness to arise. This does not have to be the case.

CHAPTER 1

EATING

How Mindfulness Helps

The process of eating is an excellent introduction to mindfulness. Even before you put food in your mouth, taste it before you actually taste. In other words, imagine the flavours, textures and temperature on your tongue before you eat it. By being present to one chewing motion at a time, you will experience even more enjoyment in the culinary delight and find that you will probably eat less and get full quicker than normal. Furthermore, mindfully chewing each mouthful approximately fifteen times will ensure better digestion of the food being consumed. If alone when eating, this technique will allow you to fully appreciate the meal and, if eating in a group, 'mindful munching' will lend itself to a more peaceful, harmonious interaction with others around the table.

The Diary

And now, the chocolate ice cream is tantalising my tastebuds as its coolness massages my entire tongue. At the same time, the cocoa impresses on the tongue tip while its sweetness ignites the sides. A squirt of saliva is timely as it assists the delightful substance to disappear down the back of my throat and into my stomach. I can still feel its coolness inside me. In the desert bowl there are two scoops remaining. The varying shades of brown and chunky bits of chocolate reflect the light from the ceiling and a nutty smell rises from the buried broken cashews. The density of the ice cream is firm as I poke the spoon into the middle of a scoop.

Unlike other more solid foods, I am even more alert to this Presence-enhancing experience by chewing less and allowing God's cold creation to simply melt in my mouth as its temperature gradually surrenders to the heat on my tongue. The silence in this moment is overshadowed by taste sensations, causing me to make ecstatic groaning noises. I try to recreate each flavoursome moment by repetitively rubbing my tastebuds on the roof of my mouth. With an appetite for several more spoonfuls, I pace myself without any rush to end this blissful experience.

And now, I am present to the powerful spice of the Japanese wasabi root. If you want to feel a sudden arising of Presence, then smear wasabi onto a piece of sushi, dip it in soy sauce and place it upside down on your tongue and commence chewing ... At this moment, as I chew a mouthful of rice, tuna, soy sauce and wasabi, an amazing sensation overcomes me. Wham! My nostrils flare and my eyes water as this ancient ground root pasty substance sends messages to my brain to wake up and become extra alert. There is no space for thought as I quickly discover there is a fine line between pleasure and pain. A gulp of cold, refreshing water is a nice palette cleanser and I now contemplate another piece of sushi decorated with the quirky green paste. This time I allow the wasabi to touch the roof of my mouth first instead of the tongue. A delay in the spice reaction occurs and is less intense than the last.

All five senses are fully engaged in togetherness as I chew slowly and deliberately to enhance the experience. My mind dares me to place an extra pinch of wasabi in between my lips to intensify the experience. So now, with the additional kick, my nostrils start dripping clear liquid as the Japanese spice does its pipe cleaning and blood purifying job most effectively.

And now, I am present to vaporizing sensations of peppermint on each inhale through the nostrils as my teeth crunch two Fisherman's Friend branded candy pieces. The flavour on my tongue is constant and unforgiving. Each breath taken in packs the most powerful punch on the throat and lungs whilst giving rise to an intense sense of Presence. My eyes are watering, fists are clenched and the senses of taste and touch are in overdrive. The youthful disposition I possess tempts me to put another two harmless-looking white mints into my mouth to relive the previous intense adventurous taste sensation. Crushing and pulverising the confectionery suddenly gives rise to the equivalent of a fireworks show exploding onto my tongue and up into my nasal passages. The main difference from the wasabi being the ice-coolness, rather than heat.

It is fascinating to note that apart from the candy-crunching sounds, everything else is muffled due to the sense of taste in the foreground working overtime. Moment by moment as the intensity gradually subsides, I become present again to the broader surroundings. A sip of cold water soothes and chills the palette and inner cheeks with a swish or two. A long, deep inhale through the nostrils forces my eyes to open wider and puts an end to a relatively cost-effective experience.

And now, the deep purple colour and vibrancy of a freshly made berry smoothie drink is jumping out at me alongside a tall glass of bright orange, carrot and ginger juice. Yes, a liquid lunch will cleanse my temple pipes. One sip at a time alternately from each glass makes me present and grateful to these antioxidant-rich beverages that are now travelling through my physical body and igniting almost orgasmic sensations of anti-ageing and bliss.

This next mouthful of smoothie reveals the drops of sweet honey I included in the mix. And this next mouthful of juice gradually exposes my tongue to the fiery ginger spice before doing its work on the inside. Placing my hands around each glass of Godly goodness and feeling a vibrant yet subtle energy, gives rise to Presence that constantly exists in plant life even after it has been pulverised in a blender. This is one of many friendly reminders of what really matters in life here on earth.

Paying attention to the assorted berries in the smoothie, I become aware of the difference in flavours between the raspberries, blueberries, blackberries, cranberries and strawberries. The texture is sometimes chewy as I negotiate a random blueberry that escaped the wrath of the blender's blade. Also each present moment is being consumed with the mild crunch between my front teeth of the tiny strawberry and blackberry seeds.

And now, having just enjoyed my mother and father's company at the Koko Black chocolatier café, I stand waiting to make payment for the coffees and hot chocolate whilst observing hundreds of varying shapes of bite size chocolate creations behind a long glass case. Nostalgia summons my inner child and my eyes widen with delight as I commence visually scanning the plethora of edible art in delicious shades of brown. On this next inhale, aromas of cocoa, cream, nuts and fruit make their way into my nostrils. I start swallowing the saliva that my glands are producing as a result of associated brain activity.

The best part about this experience is that I do not know what most of these individual ornate chocolate pieces are called. I avoid reading their small labels and instead focus on the attention to detail that makes up the content of each carefully-crafted piece. Intricate patterns and contours dress the periphery of the cocoa creations and I marvel at the mindfulness practiced by the chocolatier during the production process.

Just over there behind a glass chamber, the chocolatier dons an apron, hat and caring smile before smoothly caressing tempered liquid milk chocolate with a long silver paddle. The substance is smoothed out along a rectangular pan in preparation as the decorative layer on another darker chocolate base with half walnuts. Mmm, what an experience to savour…

Rob Ginnivan

And now, sitting patiently at a sushi train restaurant, I become mesmerized in the present moment by a number of plates gliding past on parade, displaying a variety of Japanese delicacies. The purple rice wrapped around seaweed and raw salmon jumps out at me. So with chopsticks carefully poised, I clasp the heavenly piece and proceed to dip the side in soy sauce, dab it in wasabi and place it into my mouth. A slow chewing motion ensues as I savour every flavoursome experience before it disappears into my stomach.

There exists an ongoing temptation to look ahead again at the sushi train belt for another plate while I keep chewing this piece, however I choose to lower my gaze back to the plate in front of me and savour this moment. It is fascinating to note that when I look up and become distracted with the next possible plate, the chewing experience becomes diluted and less enriching. When I return my focus to the current eating experience, the flavours and textures are amplified again.

A sip of warm green tea cleanses the palette before I consider which plate to choose next. In a playful manner, I amuse myself with the experience of looking out the window onto the street while thoughts stream into my mind. Turning my head, I regard only the sushi plates passing me by right in front of my eyes as thoughts seem to dissolve and a gap of Presence appears...

And now, my eyes scan the carefully prepared breakfast platter that is being placed on the table in the dining room. Several varieties of tropical fruit cut in juicy bite-size pieces decorate the plate. The magnificent bright colour medley of red, yellow and orange reflects the true character of fresh mango, raspberries, pineapple, plum and grapes. Firstly I taste, touch and smell the food before I place it in my mouth ... It is obvious to me that Rhonda places love, attention and creativity into the preparation of her customers' culinary delicacies. Vibrant life exists on this platter as I hold my hand just above the fruit and feel the energy of nature. The combination of mango, raspberry and plum creates a fireworks show of tanginess on my tongue, as flavours burst together in unison. And as this taste sensation begins to fade, pieces of pineapple are next in line to bring yet another wonderful experience to my temple entrance.

A time out now allows me to appreciate and savour the experience ... The light shining on the plump grapes is enough of an invitation to place one at a time into my mouth and slowly chew another fabulous creation of nature. The nutritional goodness can now be felt in parts of my body as digestion of this juicy, sweet food is well underway and feelings of euphoria emerge from within.

And now, delicately peeling the skin from a banana exposes a potassium-packed piece of white fleshy fruit. As I observe its texture and smell the flavour, the wonderment of so much goodness in one of God's great creations dawns on me. My mind marvels at its multipurpose function as a meal of its own, an energy booster, an ingredient for a cake, smoothie and so on...

The first bite has my teeth effortlessly sever the top as I gradually mash the mouthful against my tongue. Sensations of fructose sweetness emerge in this moment. An enjoyable experience is in full swing as the banana's smooth and gentle texture and flavour circulate from teeth to palette to tongue. Due to its soft consistency melting with each slow chewing motion, the opportunity to take another bite of the fruit presents itself quicker than munching on other more dense and solid fruits. Suddenly a nostalgic memory arises. A flashback of when my mother took a tray of golden brown banana cupcakes out of the oven, fresh and steaming. The temptation to eat it immediately left my tongue scalded with its heat.

And in this present moment I can feel my kidneys getting up and dancing the lambada due to the banana's potent potassium nutritional rich content.

And now, creamy cool natural Greek yoghurt is being spooned into a bowl, juicy plump walnuts are being hand-crushed and sprinkled on top, followed by a drizzle of runny honey to complete the mid-afternoon snack. I mindfully fold the nuts and golden honey into the yoghurt and observe the ingredients blending together as the colours and textures unite. The first mouthful is nothing short of spectacular, as its vibrant smell intensifies on approach. The soft crunch of broken walnut pieces complements the cooling light yoghurt overlayed with the perfect sweetness of honey.

Moments go by without words or thoughts before my stomach starts acknowledging and appreciating the goodness of this superfood concoction. Spoonful after spoonful enters my temple until there are only smears left at the bottom of the bowl. The mind starts chattering and invites me to make a second helping of this divine snack. I decide to resist its temptation, focus on the next inhale and exhale of breath, and simply rest in awareness whilst cherishing the lingering flavours and contemplating the nutritional wonder of elegant sufficiency having just been consumed.

The mind makes another attempt via my rumbling stomach to help myself to another serving of yoghurt. Amused at its potential persuasion and justification, I smile and continue to rest in Being before excusing myself from the vicinity of its ingredients.

And now, feeling suddenly peckish in the middle of the afternoon even though I have eaten a hearty breakfast and lunch, I ponder and reflect on why it is that my stomach and brain are conspiring to put more food in my physical system. The more I consider the reasons why and why not my body would require anything solid to enter the mouth, the less hungry I am actually feeling. It is interesting to observe that the initial signal from the mind to the brain was a craving for something sweet to eat. Maybe I have been resting in the stillness of a gap between thoughts for so long that the mind got bored and needed to create a distraction.

Situated now near a café that offers all sorts of delicacies entices me to confront the challenging mind and approach the café centre to simply look at what is on offer, exercise willpower, resist temptation and only order a calorie-free black coffee.

With steaming cup in hand, I waltz contently out of the establishment. I smell its aroma, feel the warmth and take the first sip. The further away geographically I become from the café, the more the original food temptation fades. Eventually it dissolves entirely. In my thoughts, words from the song 'Out of Mind Out of Sight' appear.

I smile.

Mindlessness

I remember the days when I used to mindlessly stuff my mouth with food just for the sake of filling my stomach up as quickly as possible so I could move on to the next task on my To Do list. Whilst I was taking fewer than five chews before prematurely swallowing a mouthful, I would be thinking unnecessarily about where I had to be straight after eating. Sometimes I would eat in the car while driving, with a mobile phone cradled under one ear, and talking at the same time in a muffled fashion. It is no wonder, therefore, that I would say to myself later in the day, "Did I have lunch today?" or, "Did I eat anything for breakfast?" This kind of eating without paying attention to the ritual also used to lead to indigestion, burping and heartburn. For me food was simply for survival rather than enjoyment.

Techniques to apply

And now, take a moment to consciously enjoy the next meal by paying attention to one mouthful at a time and the textures, flavours, colours, sensations and temperature that each bite involves. Chew slowly and cherish the freshness of the ingredients. Perhaps gather a few friends or family members together and announce that you are going to have some fun by creating a 'mindful meal' or 'soulful foods' experience for everyone. Encourage those at the table to take this new approach to eating, guaranteed to enhance the wellness of mind, body and soul.

CHAPTER 2

WORKING

How Mindfulness Helps

By adopting a mindfulness practice throughout the day and simply being present to each moment, working can take on a whole new meaning. Tasks that were previously difficult to perform may now be less onerous and easier to manage. And what was perceived as boring and mundane in nature can become more interesting. There is something about being attentive to the task at hand, because time takes on a whole new meaning and seems to pass by effortlessly. You could even find that eventually when being constantly mindful becomes second nature, a paradigm shift could occur and 'working' becomes such a breeze that it might be viewed with a new set of eyes as 'playing'.

The Diary

And now, sitting at the back of the boardroom among eight men dressed in dark blue suits, listening to and watching a PowerPoint presentation on the latest technology related to data storage available to the market, I start to feel sleepy and begin drifting into unconsciousness. As my head nods forward, I quickly wake up and feel a sense of Presence within my physical body and the surrounding room. My eyes start roaming around the room to observe the fine details in the floor carpet fabric, chair legs, glass windows. I feel the heat being generated from the sunlight on my skin. As I take a deeper breath in and out, I step into a deeper state of consciousness.

The presenter's speech appears as sound vibrations only, as I am oblivious to his language. Sitting on top of the stereo speaker in the front corner of the boardroom appears to be a bright red spongy stress ball.

"I wonder how long that's been there for?" I whisper to the person next to me, as if he knows.

"Six months," he replies.

With my gaze softly fixed on this new discovery, I find it enlightening to know that up until this present moment, the red object has completely bypassed my vision for several months.

Being mindful, present and paying more attention to the current surroundings in a heightened sense of awareness will assist with the observation of subtle changes and situations moving forward.

And now, the official news is that the technology company I work for has lost a major bid for a piece of business that was highly contested. A sudden sense of Presence overcomes me and I am alert to a void existing. For a fleeting moment, my physical body feels the sensation of overheating as I take a deeper breath in and out to dissolve the feeling of discomfort. I reflect on previous years before my positive transformation took place, when the reaction would have been vastly different. I imagine swearing and an increase in heartbeat would have ensued. Thank goodness for the practice of Mindfulness.

At this moment there is no second wave of discomfort and I am rather pleased about that. I marvel at how my brain has undergone some kind of neuroplasticity change over the years. I now reflect on the notion that there is a greater meaning beyond the loss of this business just experienced.

Observing others having a major, bitter reaction to the news highlights the difference in consciousness evolution. There is a look of confusion on their faces as they see me smiling and maintaining a calm disposition. There will always be other opportunities and this result is already in the past and part of history. So it is time to refocus and pay attention to what is occurring now and not five minutes ago.

And now, at home on a rainy Sunday afternoon, I am working in the garden. Because the soil is nice and moist due to the constant flow of water falling from the sky and soaking the earth, it makes it easier for each swing of the pick to strike the ground and uproot the weeds that attempt to strangle the colourful flowers. Worms and grubs scurry into holes, taking shelter from the iron pick wielding its way into the rich dark soil again and again. With water droplets falling from my eyebrows and nose tip onto a soaked T-shirt, I become aware of the wet, clinging sensation of the cotton clothing against my skin. I wriggle ten toes in my shoes and realise that so far they have been spared from any moisture and remain warm and dry.

The flower stems droop and stoop forward with the weight of the raindrops and the colours seem a lot brighter. There is an aliveness in the air as a cleansing of some kind takes place, thanks to the force of mother nature. The temptation to pick a small bright red tomato off its branch is too much to resist, so I reach over and twist it gently off the stem before placing it into my mouth. As my teeth start pulverising this Vitamin C-rich vegetable, explosions of tangy, sweet and sour flavours burst against my tastebuds and force my salivary glands to work overtime.

There is no right or wrong type of weather to be working in the garden; it is more about following the heart and finding the beauty in tidying up nature a little bit in the backyard.

And now, I am working with all three children to play and talk harmoniously together. It is challenging at times due to the vast age differences between Jesper, Annika and Oscar. The suggestion to watch a Harry

Potter movie seems to be working at the moment. This magical story relates well to the siblings on many levels. As I stand back and observe their interaction, it appears that any rivalry or differences are dissolving.

From this viewpoint there is an increased agreement about the plot development and movie characters, even laughter. The middle child, Annika, asks her brothers if they would like a piece of the chocolate cake she recently baked. Oscar moves his position to sit on his big brother's lap. Love and harmony begin to flow in abundance and their father delights at the bonding occurring.

At first I hesitate to intervene and check in to see how they are all getting along. I am guided to quietly grab a chair and sit down amongst them in front of the television. Within a few minutes the dynamics change. Dad becomes a distraction as Annika takes her attention away from her brothers and to a query about shopping in the future. After answering her question, I change my mind and decide to leave the room. Moments later, I peak into the family room to see the siblings paying full attention to each other and the adventure movie once again. Well, I am learning that trial and error sometimes needs to occur to achieve the desired outcome. In this moment they seem happy together.

And now, I am reflecting on the continual work and maintenance it takes to tame the 'wild elephant' in the mind. From simple breath work through to visualisation techniques, there is never a right or wrong way to bring the mind to a still and calm state of being. Keeping the unnecessary thoughts at bay and only entertaining the necessary thoughts is a continual work in progress.

The good news is that after persisting for a while, new habits are formed and it becomes almost effortless to be in a state of multi-dimensional consciousness. The mind is tireless and follows me wherever I go. And the amount of rest I have had, food I have eaten and circumstances I have been confronted by determines how hard the mind will work to pass comments or suggestions on a particular situation. Its deductive nature to entertain negative thoughts is being overshadowed by the positive beauty of all things and energy surrounding me. Once upon a time it was vice versa. The negative thoughts overpowered the positive ones. But with enough work, I am achieving the constant state of bliss for which I have strived on many occasions.

By repeating a mantra to myself in a transcendental meditative state, I gain access to pure consciousness with no concentration, no control of the mind, no contemplation and no monitoring of thoughts. At first this may be hard work, but after regular practice it becomes effortless.

And now, for the several thousandth time, I continue working towards keeping the receding hair on my head to a bare minimum by shaving in the shower. Precision and full attention is required with every stroke of the sharp blade across the scalp, to ensure no hair remains and the skin stays unbroken. After lathering my head with shaving cream and rinsing my hands under warm running water, I gently grip the handle of the shaver and mindfully glide it over my skin, scars and bumps towards the ear and beyond. For years I have been accustomed to this proven and effective method of hair removal. Now that the back and sides are finished, I move to the front just above the forehead, where a round patch is carefully removed with four strokes of the shaver.

Although I am not using a mirror to see what is happening moment by moment during this work in progress, there is a degree of alertness required to ensure a lapse in concentration does not result in a head cut. On this occasion I feel a small, rough patch of hair that I missed at the back. Most probably a fleeting thought that caused the blades to detour around that spot. One stroke removes it instantly. I dab the scalp with a towel a few times to remove the water before massaging a moisturiser all over the contours for a fresh, sleek feel.

And now, it is that time again to make the bed before getting on with living the day to its fullest. The sun rays are streaming into the bedroom, a cacophony of birds are heralding in another morning as I proceed to circumnavigate the bed, firstly smoothing out the creases of the under sheet. The corners and ends are covered with an elastic fitted cotton sheet and tightened. The down quilt is shaken and tossed in the air three times to evenly redistribute the feathers within. A soft breeze of air rises up against my face as the quilt lands silently on the bed. Both ends of the bed are evenly covered now with this colourful cloth.

The more I pay attention to every action associated with this daily routine, the more content and calm I feel. It is the simple tasks and regular, repeatable actions that when taken care of in the present moment, help to take my mind off the future. My hands gently puff up each side of the pillows while whistling 'The 59th Street Bridge Song (Feelin' Groovy)' by Simon & Garfunkel. A joyous heart feeling engulfs my being and I take a step back to regard the bed. I reflect on the small amount of time it took to perform this routine task. Compared to previous times of frantically making the bed in a hurry, it took approximately the same time to be mindful and deliberate with each action during this chore.

And now, the mending of a leaky bathroom tap is underway. For several weeks this supposedly tedious task has been postponed. My mind has kept telling me it will be too difficult and I won't succeed at changing the deteriorating rubber seals and replacing them with new ones. What is fascinating to note in this present moment as I mindfully unscrew the tap base with a spanner, is that the task is actually enjoyable. I am feeling confident that by continuing to pay attention to the steps required to fix this leaking tap and ignore the voice in my head, in a few minutes from now, members of this household will not have to endure the slow and constant dripping sound any longer. In fact, as a bonus, the water bill will decrease.

With precision, I reach into the tap connection with a pair of thin pliers to remove the old rubber seal and replace it with a newly purchased one. The tap parts are all screwed back together in place, the main water pump is turned back on and the faucet tested for a leak. In anticipation I softly turn the handle clockwise to a closed position and observe the flowing water come to a halt. Not a single drop emerges from the tap. The silence of the no more drip, drip, drip sound is deafening.

It now dawns on me that this handyman task took only five minutes to complete and yet the seductive mind had convinced me for weeks that it was going to take much longer and would also probably result in an accident of spraying water and injuring my finger. I will remember this valuable lesson for next time.

And now, my focus is on developing a Mindfulness Workshop series for people suffering from Post-Traumatic Stress Disorder. This year I plan to roll out six sessions that aim to gradually reduce the suffering that occurs in people who have experienced abuse or seen traumatic events unfold. In fact, this almost does not seem like work because I love being of service to others who deserve a happy, joyful and calm life.

I am experiencing a mental block against an innovative idea that will help the course material tremendously, so I put the pen down, swivel the chair around to face the window and sit still, looking outside patiently without thinking … and suddenly the idea rises out of consciousness to practice the art of laughter in each of the six sessions. With the release of happy healing hormones into the brain during the act of laughter, I am getting a strong sense that this will be beneficial to the workshop attendees.

And another idea surfaces now to enhance the previous idea. I decide to include a symbol that will trigger off the fit of laughter each time it is seen. This is the reverse of what occurs when certain triggers activate the brain to react against a traumatic memory. The 'laughter activation' symbols may be some things that can be seen often in everyday life, like a car steering wheel, pot, fork, toilet bowl, slice of bread, the sky, shoes or a mobile phone.

And now, I am on the telephone to make a reservation at a secluded Bed & Breakfast accommodation site down at the South Coast. This is so I can work in solitude on the completion of the book you are currently reading. A friendly voice answers the phone and starts to inform me of the wonderful room facilities and cost per night. Making conversation, Karen, the hotel manager, asks me the purpose of my visit.

"I need some time away to finish writing a book," I respond enthusiastically.

"Oh, is that a book that I might read?" Karen asks.

"Yes, of course it is!" I respond.

Without even knowing what this book is about, she says she would like to read it once it is published.

And then she goes on to say that even not knowing what this book is about, it is going to be interesting and inspiring!

Karen continues to delight me by saying that she will ensure there is a desk in the room to write at, and asks if I will need a charger for my laptop computer. I say that the book is being handwritten first before electronically typed. Karen is amused and remarks how great it is to see an author writing in the good old-fashioned way: with 'soul'. I am deeply grateful for everything on offer including several ink pens on the desk before my arrival.

This high level of care and hospitality is to be acknowledged and promoted to everyone in the industry of customer service.

Mindlessness

Many years before adopting a regular mindfulness practice, I used to associate working with pain and suffering; a chore that had to be done and not enjoyed. My firm belief system was that working was associated with trading time for money on an hourly rate and a boss who was forever correcting me during the tasks. Because of this, my mind would embellish the story associated with working and I would become resentful, bitter, unmotivated and overthinking situations whilst constantly wishing the hours away so I could go home. This unfortunately led to me being lazy and taking shortcuts, and finding ways to cheat the system.

Techniques to Apply

Form a new habit to be consciously present in every moment to situations that you consider working. Pay attention to each and every task and minimise the distractions of the chattering mind. Find something interesting about each work task you perform. In a non-judgemental way, write down a work situation you were involved in and pay attention to documenting the details of the people involved, task being performed, and its results.

CHAPTER 3

LOVING

How Mindfulness Helps

When you keep an open and still mind, and view people and surroundings in a non-judgemental way whilst looking for the beauty instead of the problem, an increased sense of love enters your being. In this loving state, 'feel good' sensations start to ripple throughout your physical body. It is fascinating to then observe how your surroundings respond back to you favourably. People smile at you more; nature looks, feels and sounds better; you begin to be of service to others in a compassionate sense; and there is an underlying vibration of a unity of consciousness that eventually reveals itself amongst the universal environment in which we all live.

Rob Ginnivan

Diary

And now, enjoying father and daughter time with thirteen-year-old Annika as her shopping bag carrier, I mindlessly follow her as she swans in and out of clothing stores, book shops, jewellery and make-up stands. We stop at a café to take a break and enjoy a hot chocolate with marshmallows and a coffee. She looks me in the eyes and says, "I love you Dad," and gives me a big hug. I cherish the moment and absorb her loving vibes. Then my mind asks whether it is just because I bought her several items in this vast shopping mall? Instead I accept that Annika truly loves me and is grateful that we take time out together to bond as parent and child.

We continue to smile at each other in silence, sipping our hot drinks as a beautiful feeling of limbic resonance infuses my soul with an abundance of love. The gratitude I feel to have been part of creating this wonderful human being who operates at a higher state of consciousness never ceases to amaze me. We take a deep breath in together and leave the café for more shopping.

As we walk past a charity coin box for less fortunate people, Annika stops, pulls out her pocket change and proudly drops the coins in the slot, then picks up the pace again on a mission for a pair of jeans shorts. This random act of kindness makes me joyous and full of love for her humanitarian consideration at the tender age of thirteen.

And now, nine-year-old Oscar is upset because his bluetongue lizard, Lucky, has escaped from the cage and disappeared into the backyard.

"We must find him NOW!" exclaims Oscar. His love for this reptile is obvious and I feel sorrow for him in a state of despair as we scurry, searching amongst the bushes. At the same time, I am happy for Lucky, who is free to roam around in nature. Together, the whole family systematically combs the backyard in hope of finding the lizard.

It is insightful to witness the greater detail of nature and its associated energy as I get down on my stomach and start looking at eye level to grasshoppers and blades of grass, in search of the much-loved reptile. Sounds are amplified down here close to the earth's surface as I hear rustling noises in the bushes that normally would not be noticed.

Smells of sweet flower pollen jump out at my nostrils as bees hover, taking their share from in between petals. After searching high and low, the sun begins its descent behind the hill, making visibility harder. We decide to call off the search until tomorrow. A sad-faced Oscar leaves a piece of banana on a plate outside Lucky's cage, just in case he makes his way back to captivity all by himself. I give Oscar a loving hug of sympathy on the way back into the house.

And now, Oscar randomly announces to me, "I love you, Dad, you are the best father a boy could have!" We smile and embrace. This incredible child has the wisdom of Solomon, a heart of gold and is well beyond his years on this earth. Thank God I postponed that vasectomy ten years ago.

Following our expression of father/son love for each other, we return to the golf game. As Oscar's caddy, I remove the sand wedge from the buggy and hand it to him. With the ball in the bunker, he is determined to chip it up, out and over onto the putting green with one strike. He is adorable to watch being in the now, as the concentration on his face and intensity in his eyes focus on the task at hand. Like a meerkat, he extends his neck and raises his head above the edge of the putting green to see the hole. It appears his ambition is grander that I thought. The ball does not make it out on the first strike. Oscar takes a deep breath in and out before gracefully striking the ball a second time and lobbing it over the edge. It rolls down the slopping green within inches of the hole.

"Putting wedge please, Dad," Oscar demands. I place all my attention on visualising the golf ball rolling into the hole on his first attempt. He taps the ball gently and it circles the hole's edge once before falling in. We give each other a high five hand slap and move on to the next fairway.

And now, the children are waking up to the first day of the new school year. I make my way downstairs and into the kitchen to pack their lunches. Paying attention to the spreads and fillings to be placed in between the fresh bread slices, I mindfully distribute Nutella evenly across to each corner of each slice. With love, I close the sandwiches and proceed to carefully cut off the crusts on all sides without removing any of the chocolate spread. To ensure the sandwiches remain soft and intact, I gently place them into hard containers and slot a shiny red apple into the corresponding compartments. The tangy smell and bright colour of the chilled orange juice alerts me to this fruit's goodness as I pour it into the children's thermal flasks.

With the best intentions for Annika and Oscar, I seal the lunches with a prayer for a smooth and wonderful day at school before placing them into each respective bag. Nothing goes to waste as the cut bread crusts are tossed into the dog's food bowl for inspection and potential devouring.

It is now interesting to note that due to the mindfulness applied during the lunch-making ritual this morning, there is less mess to clean up on the kitchen bench. Two swipes of a wet cloth across the bench top sees it returned to the original tidy state it was greeted in at first.

And now, David is playing the cello live right here in a yoga meditation class. The harmonics from this beautiful instrument reverberate in every corner of

Tidy Temple Yoga studio. When David caresses the strings with the bow on a low note, I feel the sound vibrate in my heart. When he draws the bow across a high note, I feel it in my head.

The soulful nature with which the cellist makes love with the strings tied to the dark varnished hollow wood body, is permeating into the class attendees, and I glance across the studio to observe people almost melting into their yoga mats in full, surrendering relaxation. A state of blissful unity fills the room as some faces are smiling and others show tears of joy and some sadness.

The final piece being played invokes melancholic memories. Flashes of past good times all the way back to childhood arise. When we are asked to sit up in a cross-legged position to enjoy the silence after the cello strums its final note, I feel an overwhelming sense of Presence in true ecstatic harmony. I want to stay here in this seated position for much longer as the vibration from the string instrument continues to resound in each and every cell of my body ... I am the last in class to get up and pack my yoga mat away. As people move around to conclude the class, I can feel the strength of the subtle vibration dissipate, dissolve and eventually disappear within the studio space.

And now, taking an evening promenade down a bush trail, I am present to the love and beauty all around me. And for the first time in my life I actually stop to hug the next tall gumtree. With my arms wrapped around its base, I start feeling an energetic vibration of unity between us. I clasp my hands and rest my cheek on it and simply remain in Being. This is so beautiful. Sensations, images and feelings continue surfacing. The strength and stability of the wood circumference reminds me of when I was just a young child hugging my father's leg. A few black ants crawl onto my skin to investigate the situation. The sensation is ticklish and forces me to break out in laughter.

Then right on cue, the song 'Love Is In The Air' resounds in my head.

A sense of remorse suddenly builds inside my physical body and tears cascade down my cheeks, as I recall chopping down several trees with a chainsaw over two decades ago when I was working for a tree lopper to make enough cash to feed my family. I apologise to nature for what I now consider to be an unconscious act and continue mindfully strolling down the dirt trail, feeling a sense of closure and a lightness of being.

And now, just outside the deck of the beach house, a curious kangaroo decides to query the stillness of my being in meditation whilst overlooking the mesmerising ocean waves. At first I ignore the fluffy marsupial and continue to rest in awareness, however it approaches so close to me, I can now feel the warm, grassy breath from its soft nostrils against my hands. As its inspection of this strange, still human continues, I decide to get up out of the chair slowly and reposition myself cross-legged on the ground.

Ever curious, Kangaroo rubs its lips on the crown of my bald head. The sensation is ticklish and sends shivers down my spine. I start wondering if it is enjoying the salty sweat on my skin.

Another beautiful connection with nature as I remain almost as still as a statue to receive this love and attention from a furry creature. I dare not move in case Kangaroo becomes startled. Thinking is kept to a minimum too, as it may send out foreign vibes to the sensitively-conscious marsupial. So I continue to increase the focus on each and every one of my breaths.

Eventually it hops away and I feel a heightened sense of alertness and Presence. The smell of fresh poo wafts by my nose with the sea breeze as I look down to see Kangaroo has left me with a steaming souvenir shaped like dark pebbles.

And now, I see in the distance an old high school friend for the first time in over thirty years. My breath deepens and sensations of butterflies enter my stomach region. As I approach her in the street, a flashback image in my mind surfaces of when the two of us left school without saying goodbye to each other. The song angels now flood my mind with the Cat Stevens song, '(Remember The Days Of The) Old Schoolyard'. No wonder I am feeling these sensations. My mind intervenes again and asks if there was any unfinished business.

So I am present right here to a big reuniting hug from Lisa. The embrace has a feeling of harmonious chemistry similar to that from decades ago. It is immediately evident that she is distracted with something other than this present moment. As she speaks, her eyes are constantly looking over my shoulder and to both sides. When I start talking and asking about her life since we last saw each other, she replies, at the same time checking her Facebook status on her handheld device. She now asks me if it's okay if she replies to an email.

It seems to me we have both evolved at different stages. From memory, Lisa's behaviour back in high school was very much in the present moment and paying attention to one task at a time, contrary to this present moment, where multi-tasking and divided attention seem to dominate. I understand that she may not have yet been exposed to the practice of mindfulness, so I remain loving, patient and understanding to her current way of being.

And now, being walked by the family dog, Stella, as she pulls me forward on her leash almost choking herself, I sense love in the air. Up ahead is another dog of the same breed, catching the attention of Stella.

Whimpering and howling, she leads me across the other side of the road where her kind awaits with tail wagging. Their noses touch, both tails thrash frantically and there seems to be a genuine loving connection as they sniff each other's backsides and follow each other around in a tight circle.

Dogs live in the present moment and I relish the bonding occurring between these two four-legged canines. It is fascinating that all attention from both dog owners is on the movement and interaction between Stella and Haley. There is obvious communication taking place independent of any spoken words. The odd snort, sniff and sudden head movement appears to be enough body language to tell each other the latest news and indicate they have a connection beyond human understanding.

This all-too-brief encounter comes to an end as the dogs part company and are no longer interested in each other. As they walk in opposite directions, neither bothers to look back at the other.

And now, sitting in the waiting area of a dental surgery, I am present to the love a mother is sharing with her baby. From its pram, the infant gurgles and smiles up at the mother. The woman whispers sweet murmuring sounds back to her baby. A beautiful loving communication is taking place independent of words of formal language and it is evident that an intimate understanding of each other is in progress. Various exchanges of smiles, sounds and other facial expressions transpire for several minutes.

The limbic resonance between mother and child transfers invisibly across to me as I smile in delight, witnessing their love. As I look around at three other people sitting next to me, I notice that they too are charmed by the correspondence between the parent and child. I step outside the waiting area for a breath of fresh air and notice a completely different vibe and energy as cars drive by and people rush around in a state of 'doing'.

When I step back into the room, a sense of unity, peace, calm and harmony is present. This is a nice place to rest in Being for a while longer. Amusing to note that there do not appear to be any signs of nervousness from anyone else waiting to be seen by the dentist.

Mindlessness

Previously I thought 'loving' was reserved for hippies, people in a romantic relationship, and babies and their mothers. So I would approach situations with a Fight or Flight mentality, factual outlook, and black and white assessment full of judgements and assumptions. For example, I would identify with my mind and ignore feelings in a situation where there was a person I did not get along with. If this person fell over and hurt themselves, I would laugh to myself, ignore them, and walk away without giving a hand up, hoping they had hurt themselves in the process. It wasn't until much later and having been enlightened, that I realised even if you don't like someone, it is still possible to love and provide assistance when in need.

Techniques to Apply

Next time you see someone whom you normally feel awkward being near, throw them a warm smile by lifting the muscles in both corners of the mouth even if you don't feel like it. Find an example of living in loving moments you have encountered and reflect on the sensations, images, feelings and thoughts it enriched you with.

CHAPTER 4

GIVING

How Mindfulness Helps

The more mindful you are, the more generous with your time and money you become towards people and living creatures less fortunate. Over time, the act of 'giving' becomes effortless and eventually joyful. The sense of fulfilment being of service to others brings subtly creeps into the state of Being and acts of Doing. In turn, you will find that the universe will return the goodness back to you many times over as a result of your act of kindness. And sometimes you discover that the smallest and least time-consuming random act of giving results in the biggest positive impact on the situation.

The Diary

And now, I am feeling a great sense of Presence in contemplation at Remembrance Day. A rising energy of 'giving' surfaces from within and I decide to donate my Eckhart Tolle premier seat tickets to one of the wounded warriors who put his life on the line to protect the country and defend others who were under siege and needed help. Like a lotus flower blooming, an overwhelming sense of satisfaction expands from my inside out. I cannot wipe the smile off my face as I reflect on how wonderful it feels to give back to others who have also helped people – especially those who were injured in the process.

Knowing the wisdom and inspiration that Eckhart gives people from all walks of life in varying circumstances, makes it beyond question to give up my ticket to someone who will benefit, potentially transforming another life in the right direction.

So with enthusiasm, I pick up the phone and send a message to one of Soldier On's former serving commandos to offer the ticket. It is exhilarating as I now wait in anticipation to hear if this brave person is available on the evening to attend a monumental event.

And now, I am on an airplane to go meet His Holiness The 14th Dalai Lama and attend his teachings of the Heart Sutra and Eight Verses of Mind Training. A few rows in front of me, a monk sits in the aisle seat. A sense of knowing arises, as I believe he is also going to attend the seminar today. As soon as the seat belt lights dim, I walk down the plane aisle to introduce myself. He greets me with a very peaceful half Buddha smile.

"Are you going to Quang Minh Temple to attend the teachings of His Holiness?" I ask softly.

With an enthusiastic nod of his bald head, the monk asks if I would like a ride from the airport to the temple.

"Well, how about I save you some money and you ride with me in a taxi?" I suggest.

"I asked you first!" The monk smiles in gratitude.

But now my mind intervenes and causes a bodily sensation of awkwardness and embarrassment as if to say to me, *You are only imposing if you take up the offer to hitch a ride with the monk!*

At this moment, the Buddhist looks me in the eyes warmly and cheerfully exclaims, "The gift is in the giving! You must come with me in my car."

I am honoured and humbly take up the offer, return to my seat and wait patiently for the flight to complete its path before landing.

And now, standing in the supermarket queue waiting to be served and process a few grocery items, the confident voice of a jolly man behind me bellows at the prospect of Christmas approaching. As the intermittent beeping sound of the cashier's scanner acknowledges the registration of each product, I spy a charity box at the checkout counter raising money for kids with cancer. I reach into my pocket and remove all available coins, then place them in the fundraising box. The cashier greets me with a smile and starts processing my grocery items, only to discover that the large portion of fresh salmon I am cooking for dinner tonight is not scanning properly.

In frustration, she rings the bell for Customer Assistance to identify the error on the barcode for the $25 purchase. Meanwhile, due to the delay, a growing line of restless shoppers awaits alongside the conveyer belt in anticipation of a quicker resolution. I maintain a calm and content disposition. The jolly man right behind me tells the young cashier: "Just type this code into the cash register, process the salmon at zero cost and keep going with the next customer."

Incredibly grateful, I turn around to acknowledge the man's generosity of living by the spirit of the law rather than the letter of the law, and observe the name badge on his lapel bears the title Shift Supervisor. Well, I guess the gift is in the giving.

And now, out of the corner of my eye I notice lovely neighbour, Monica, approaching our front door and mindfully placing several recently picked vegetables on the doormat. I observe her carefully lay down bright yellow and dark green zucchinis; luscious, plump red tomatoes; and light green snow peas. She smiles to herself and quietly tiptoes away back to her house. A sense of gratitude rises within me and I feel extremely fortunate and loved. I take another few moments to digest what has just occurred, then proceed to gather the organically grown goodies and bring them inside and onto the kitchen bench. It is wondrous to note that the act of giving from the kind next-door neighbour can be felt in my hands along with the vibrant energy transferred from the universe's great edible creations.

Well there is nothing like the Now, so I start chopping the vegetables and place them into a pot of water along with a stock cube for additional flavour. Within minutes I am blending the softened veggies and broth into a sumptuous soup. The flavours start jumping out of the bowl; I can taste the food before I actually place the first spoonful into my mouth.

Mmm, nothing like a bowl of fresh organic vegetable soup. The aroma and colours are simply divine. A sprinkle of Himalayan pink rock salt and a splash of virgin olive oil complete the experience.

And now, I am sitting with and being of service to one of Australia's war veteran heroes, Todd – a soldier who put his life on the line several years ago on tour in East Timor. The guided meditation session and mindfulness practice I am taking this wounded warrior through is aimed to relieve the Post-Traumatic Stress Disorder he still suffers. Leading with compassion and care, I mention that the past does not exist anymore and the future is unknown.

What exists right now is the present moment. There follows a wordless acknowledgement from Todd that he has faith in what I am teaching.

In this moment, together we broaden our awareness by shifting attention to the five senses of smell, sound, sight, taste and touch. A stoic, peaceful and powerful energy emanates from Todd as he puts his trust in the techniques of stilling the mind and focusing on the body. I am conscious that sweet smells can trigger off unpleasant memories of decaying flesh and debilitating bodily sensations. Our breath is synchronised as I silently send the best intentions for internal peace over to the former soldier.

Todd leaves our session feeling centred and at peace with a deeper sense of calm. It is with great honour that I can donate my time and play a part in the healing of this brave person.

And now, Oscar, dressed up as Santa Claus, is distributing gifts to his family sitting around the lounge room. He mindfully arranges the parcels in piles with a slight grin on his face in anticipation of a giving exercise unfolding moment by moment.

This generous, unassuming, considerate and highly conscious person commences proceedings by giving his parents their gifts first. The look of love in his eyes as he carefully hands over the presents is heart-warming. His elder brother's turn is next. Oscar removes the largest gift from Jesper's pile and rushes it over to him with excitement. Then his sister Annika finally receives her gift, as Oscar is a bit shy when he hands it to her.

Later on, I help Oscar clean his bedroom and put toys away. His wallet is sitting on the study desk, looking rather empty. Knowing how heavy and full the wallet used to be before Christmastime, I pick it up and briefly inspect the contents, to find it completely empty. Thinking of others before himself, this amazing boy spent all his money on gifts for family members. He tells me it felt really good to give to others and see them smile so much.

In this moment, I rest in awareness of a truly evolving young human being making a positive difference in the little time he has had so far on this earth.

And now, it feels fulfilling to be at a senior citizens' retirement village, helping out and volunteering services. There is a strong vibe of enlightenment among the patrons here. As I walk through the main dining hall, faces light up with warm, glowing smiles as my shiny bald head is inspected by some. I remember at this moment what Eckhart Tolle said at a retreat about the ageing physical form: As the body deteriorates physically, there is a rise in Consciousness and Presence. Although the majority of people here have frail and fragile bodies, there is a noticeably soulful sparkle in their eyes. I bring water and cups of tea to the elder generation and sit talking to a few.

Through conversation, I am awakening to the peaceful and joyful disposition most of these men and women display whilst surrendering to the earth and knowing this communal home may be their last in this human form. One lady reaches out to hold my hand. Upon contact with her, I feel a real sense of cosmic and soul consciousness. Biologically she is ninety-eight years. Yet she still portrays a playful youthfulness about her. The energy that I can feel in Margaret's hand is the same energy I feel in my children's hands.

In this present moment, I am alert to the situation that I may never see some of these senior citizens again on this earth, as I wave goodbye, walking out of the premises.

And now, in church I observe a senior citizen of the local community stand at the end of each aisle, giving his time to collect money in the small wicker basket that makes its way, hand-to-hand, systematically past each person for donations. His face appears to have an inner glow behind the many creases and deep wrinkles. Since I was a young boy some forty years ago, I can remember this very same man engaged in this service at each Mass I attended.

His being of service time after time each Sunday is playing a part of preserving the longevity of the human form God has given him. It is delightful to witness his weekly routine of collecting funds to assist the church with those less fortunate. There appears to be a permanent smile on his face as he methodically takes the basket at the end of each aisle and shuffles over to the next one.

A genuine sense of satisfaction adorns this physically frail being and I wonder about the ability and deeper meaning of consistently dedicating himself to the weekly task. The way he mindfully takes the collection basket from one churchgoer and passes it to the next is performed with the utmost grace and gratitude. The priest also spares a smile of admiration for this wonderful soul covered up in human form.

And now, the stop light at a major intersection in Manila brings the car to a halt. A young child with bare feet, no shirt and torn short pants approaches my window with tired eyes and hand held out, asking for money. My heart deepens with sorrow and compassion, as I roll down the window to give the boy a bottle of water and packet of assorted nuts.

I am present to knowing that it is better for him to receive nutrition and sustenance rather than money. The reason being that unfortunately the money he receives will only be collected by a syndicate at the end of the day. As the young boy takes the food and drink from me, his face lights up with a smile from ear to ear. I look at him in the eyes and, with a smile, say, "God bless you."

As the car window rolls up, I watch the boy run surreptitiously behind a tree, open the water bottle for a quick drink and place a handful of nuts in his mouth. The traffic light turns green and I slowly accelerate. Glancing in the rear view mirror, I catch the boy waving goodbye to me. In this present moment, I feel a sense of gratitude and at the same time, say a prayer for his survival, safety and freedom.

And now, sitting around the dining table, it becomes apparent that I have not cooked enough chicken drumsticks for the family members and their ravenous appetite at this evening's dinner. So I view this an upside opportunity to limit my meat intake, spontaneously eat a vegetarian diet and offer up my drumsticks to the children. There is no hesitation as I announce that I am not really that hungry tonight.

Also, there is less orange juice than I thought and I start to question my planning of grocery items for this current weekend. So I mention that a glass of water is all I want to quench my thirst right now

Now & Now

and anyone else at the table is welcome to my juice. Still, the urban myth, 'bad things happen in threes', torments my mind and sure enough, we are running low on ice cream for dessert.

I surrender the chocolate ice cream serving to Annika, a self-confessed chocoholic, and make up the excuse that I am now trying to lose more weight for a running event I am planning to enter in the next few weeks. I am viewed suspiciously now. It seems all too coincidental to those around the table and suddenly the tides turn as I am being offered food from others in sympathy for my selflessness and me.

Mindlessness

In years gone by, without even consciously knowing it, I would have been selfish and greedy with time and money. My old belief system would have been to look after myself. Only if I had a little spare time or pocket change, would I even think about helping others. I was so mindless at times that I would blatantly ignore a crisis situation right under my nose and listen to the voice in my head saying, *Don't worry, someone else will come along and help this poor bastard out of this mess.*

57

Techniques to apply

In a reflective or meditative state, ask yourself the question, "How can I best be of service?" and, rather than look for the answer, simply let go. The answer will present itself to you in time. Also, the next time you put yourself in a giving situation, be sure to journal how your act of kindness helps others and enriches yourself and others around you.

CHAPTER 5

CREATING

How Mindfulness Helps

I t is fascinating to experience an increase in creativity over a period of time following a regular meditation and mindfulness practice. And you don't have to be an experienced meditator to reap the creative benefits. According to a number of studies, the findings support the belief that meditation can have a long-lasting influence on human cognition, including how we give birth to new ideas. After experiencing a consistent practice of living in the present moment, don't be surprised if innovative solutions to long-term problems arise out of 'left field'. From time to time the idea may even be radical.

The Diary

And now, inside the university Co-Op food market and cafe, I wait for a coffee and homemade vegetarian pie to be delivered to the table. There seems to be no hurry from the waitress or the barista making the drink. And this is just fine with me, because it is refreshing being in the Presence of the relaxing atmosphere here.

Whilst observing the creative surroundings, I am present to people dressed in colourful garments, walls featuring modern art, meditative music with a fusion of eclectic sounds, unusual herbal aromas, bohemian furniture and containers bursting with a variety of fresh organic food.

What becomes apparent to me as my brain's creative juices start percolating, is that there are almost no labels on anything in this establishment and that most things in this atmosphere are unfamiliar. So it is no wonder that heightened awareness and alertness is moving through my physical body more than usual.

A sense of peace and contentment encourages my inner child to play as I gaze at my surroundings like a boy. Students arrive on bicycles, swan around, sip their hot drinks while studying and give out a general vibe that life is great. It is evident in this creative place that there are very few boundaries.

And now, I am present to a heated argument between a man and woman standing outside a bus stop. They are shouting at each other and making obscene hand gestures. I cannot understand what they are saying but I know that the situation may worsen, so I decide to walk towards the bus stop and sit on the bench nearby.

As I walk past, I make eye contact with both parties and smile. They lower their voices a few decibels in response. Their body language calms as I sit, consciously creating loving vibes of harmony for this troubled couple. They look over at me, appearing to feel apprehensive about their actions. I smile warmly and say, "Hi". Within seconds, both man and woman completely stop talking and take a seat next to me. In silence now, I glance over at them to see that they are holding hands and being very still.

Miraculously, I feel a serene sense of Presence and start to wonder how this situation became diffused so quickly. Eventually a bus arrives and the couple hop on, making their way to sit down. I remain sitting on the bench when the bus drives off and feel a lingering vibe of turbulent energy surrounding me. I reflect on the calmness amidst chaos that only moments ago may have turned nasty.

I am not sure what it all means, but it is what it is. I am grateful that the intelligence of intuition led me into this situation.

Now with a heightened state of consciousness, radical creativity arises within and gives birth to my new idea of conducting the world's first airborne yoga and meditation class in a hot-air balloon. And of course there is a compassionate meaning behind the proposed stunt – a fundraising event to raise money for those suffering from Post-Traumatic Stress Disorder and a crusade for suicide prevention.

With a strong feeling of Presence, I bear witness to an increase in energy and invigoration to action this groundbreaking idea. Yes, from my memory of becoming the first person to run a half marathon in a hot-air balloon in May 2012, I recall the dimensions of the basket. It perfectly fits two yoga mats and a compartment for the pilot and gas bottles.

After approaching a highly decorated contemporary war veteran affected by his service, with an invitation to be my student during this radical fundraising stunt, I gain his commitment to perform in this event.

So now, Todd and I are rehearsing the yoga and meditation sequence in the hot-air balloon basket at ground level. Mindfully we agree that the poses being performed on the day will be synonymous with stillness, peace and confidence. It is an honour to be in the Presence of a human being so passionate about helping the lives of others in need.

And now, I am finalising the composition of a guided meditation album titled *Renew U*. From nothingness, and inspired by attending a recent Eckhart Tolle retreat, this creation is just flowing out of awareness effortlessly beyond thought. And just somehow knowing what society would like to help them shift consciousness on mass, I am compelled to produce this album and make it accessible to all. It staggers me that words simply flow from the pen onto paper and then through the harmonics of my voice with a background of gentle, soothing music.

The variety of eleven meditation tracks accompanied by various instrumental pieces geared to assist human beings access the power of Presence and higher states of consciousness, makes it a sheer pleasure to be of service to humanity. The more I create, the more I am able to create! It is deeply enriching to invent such a service for others to enjoy and be enlightened by. Rehearsing each narrative track with background music puts me into a cosmic state of bliss. And also thanks to the wisdom I learnt from Deepak Chopra at his Journey to Enlightenment retreat, it is without effort I am accessing a fraction of those infinite possibilities and ways to communicate them to society at large.

And it fascinates me that listening to my guided meditation tracks can instantly elevate me above the canvas of the thinking mind without feeling awkward that I am listening to my own recorded voice.

And now, to add some more colour and plant life to the house, I am strolling through the neighbourhood and surrounding bush trails at the crack of dawn, picking an assortment of flowers. It is fascinating to note that when one's attention is focussed on a specific theme, the broader awareness gives rise to noticing more than would be ordinarily observed. It is amazing me just how many varieties and shades of colours exist of these joyous God-given floral creations.

I like the fact I do not even know the names of most of these flowers. It is actually keeping me in the present moment and away from unnecessary thinking. These scissors are useful to snip the base of the flower stems effortlessly. People walk past me, smiling with delight at the growing bunch of flowers draped over my forearm. This is a fun exercise, creating a floral arrangement for my abode.

Back at the house now, the collected assortment of colours and fragrances are being mindfully split into smaller bunches for placement in the kitchen, bedrooms and living room. A new vibe of joy and life ripples through the place, as flowers decorate benches and tables. I liken the experience to flicking on a 'colour switch' in each room.

And now, Annika is in her element as she mindfully melts and tempers a block of chocolate in preparation for some intricate sculptures with which to dress this evening's ice cream desert. It is lovely to witness such creativity blossom within a young teenager. The smell of the cocoa travels through the air and into my nostrils as the glistening confectionery liquefies in the bowl. Annika opens a piping bag for the melting chocolate to be poured into before the edible art starts flowing onto the tray.

As I observe every delicate movement of the liquid chocolate forming all kinds of intricate shapes whilst escaping the pointy end, the sense of Presence arises, expressing itself as warm tingling sensations down from my neck to the base of the spine. The sculptures Annika is designing with this chocolate are unlike anything I have seen before. For a moment my finger has a mind of its own and makes its way into the bowl for a quick dip before entering my mouth for a sampling. Salivary glands swing into action to assist the tasting experience.

A leaf plucked from a backyard tree branch is now being used as the mould for wafer thin chocolate decorations. My mind is dancing around, ready to take control of my hand and pick up a chocolate sculpture for immediate consumption. A deep breath in and a deep breath out brings me back to the present moment of observation only.

And now, family friends proudly show me a painting that their eldest teenage daughter created in Canada. Immediately I am drawn into the canvas and become more and more curious at its surreal multi-dimensional aspects of depth, colour, light and themes across the portrait landscape. In the foreground are several teardrop-shaped rock boulders with small orange lantern lights at the base, glowing from inside a window. A wall of trees separates the boulders from a backdrop of skyscraper buildings against a dusk sky. My perception evolves to interpret the art piece as a representation of elements of earth and its human race creation fused with that of another planet of some kind.

In the bottom left hand corner is a frail young girl, barefoot and holding a lantern. She is making her way towards the boulders in search of something. I feel extremely present and alert, and sense the wonderment of a child surfacing at the mystery surrounding this creative feast. There seems to be a theme of discovery here and my curiosity intensifies. The artist's parents now tell me that their daughter has experienced a number of life challenges of recent times and seems to be moving past them successfully, and is on a recovery path. My interpretation of the artist's motivation to create such a masterpiece is that by expressing herself with a paintbrush on canvas, that this may be a way of journeying towards self-actualisation.

And now, I sit on a bench in the botanical gardens, intermittently opening and closing my eyes in stillness. Non-actively listening to the surroundings and simply enjoying the ever increasing length of each gap between thoughts, I create space for something new; ready to receive creative ideas and moments of clarity.

With pen and paper handy, I jot down each idea as it surfaces out of consciousness. This is fascinating and so much fun. Time dissolves and I have no idea what time it actually is at this moment. I do know that I am present to daylight and a shining sun. In fact, the less thoughts come and go, the more radically creative the ideas are that arise. An example of an idea that bubbled up to the surface just now, is to make a highly nutritious anti-ageing energy snack bar containing twelve superfood ingredients like oats, blueberries, quinoa, honey, pecan nuts, dark chocolate, pomegranate, orange peel, yoghurt, pumpkin and chia seeds and walnuts, and call it, 'Tidy My Temple'.

Another idea is to travel across Australia and America in a caravan, stopping at 100 towns in 100 days and teaching Mindfulness and shifting consciousness, in the process raising money for research and support centres for sufferers from Post-Traumatic Stress Disorder. Hmm, let's see what else will arise next by sitting still in silence…

And now, in the middle of the town square during the annual multicultural festival, I see a young man holding up a cardboard sign with the words, *FREE HUGS*. He has a permanent welcoming smile on his face as he periodically rotates his body in all directions with the sign clearly visible to catch the attention of passers-by.

I sense his authenticity. In these present moments, mostly females are stopping for a free hug. It seems he is creating an opportunity for anyone in need of human contact to have a quick pit stop, and feel the love and unity connection before moving on. It is fascinating that each hug is brief and very seldom words or eye contact is exchanged. At the same time it is amusing to see people happy and reenergised from giving a complete stranger a hug. I become alert to a growing number of bystanders like myself simply observing this display of creative human affection and openness to others.

One hour later, I return to the *FREE HUGS* stand to see the same man still standing in the same spot with his offer of free affection. What I find most interesting now, is that there are no hidden agendas or ulterior motives of solicitation at the end of each hug.

And now, the creation of a montage in a slide show with music overlayed provides nostalgic entertainment. My younger sister, Natasha, is being celebrated for her forty-fifth birthday. I have discovered the best way to choose the most meaningful pictures of her life evenly spaced over the years since infancy, is to sift through a few photos at a time, put them down, close my eyes, resting in awareness, until one or two pictures that really resonate jump out at me.

It is only when I actively think which one of the photos is going to be suitable for the birthday montage that I can't make up my mind. I am alert to the experience that creating is spontaneous in most cases and there appears to be no rhyme or reason why this occurs, other than the rising of a form of intelligence that is seemingly beyond the rational mind.

At this present moment, my mind tries to seduce me with the traumatic time as children when I chased Natasha down the house hallway until she accidentally put her arm through a door, shattering glass and sustaining deep cuts in her flesh. Rather than scratch that itch by indulging the thought further, I acknowledge that the past does not exist anymore whilst taking a deep inhale and exhale to bring my brain back online, ready for the next creative moment.

Mindlessness

Once upon a time, I saw everything in black and white, logically and without any room or tolerance for imagination. Without a mindfulness practice, I was constantly consumed with impatience to get the job done and move into the future. What this did was stifle any chance of creativity surfacing. I very seldom took a few moments out to simply sit still, look, listen and reflect on a situation. In 'think tank' or 'brain storming' sessions to come up with new ideas, I often found myself unable to contribute. My mind just drew mental blanks. It was frustrating and it wasn't until I had developed a regular meditation and mindfulness practice that I realised the creative limitations I had been placing on myself for so many years.

Techniques to Apply

Be patient with yourself as you take a few minutes a day out of your busy schedule to simply sit in stillness. Pay attention to one breath at a time. Take some time out to create something new that you are unfamiliar with and write about each step taken during the creation.

CHAPTER 6

DRIVING

How Mindfulness Helps

The first and most obvious advantage of being mindful and not distracted when driving is to not crash the vehicle and avoid harm to yourself and others. Having both hands on the steering wheel and resisting the temptation to check Facebook, email or make a telephone call, will minimise the risk of accidents. And by paying attention to the surroundings inside and outside of the vehicle, how you are feeling on the drive and being aware of the road ahead, can make for a more pleasant and interesting experience, especially if the journey is long. Also, if you are not the one driving, it pays to be aware of the driver. Being mindful whilst driving and not taking offence to an impatient or reckless driver will minimise road rage as well.

The Diary

And now, the road ahead is straight, flat and long. As far as the eye can see, it does not seem to change despite the car travelling at great speed. The only indications that I am getting somewhere are the trees on each roadside moving quickly past my peripheral vision. The mind starts wanting to engage in all kinds of chatter – both wild and tame. I am not interested in engaging it in thought at the moment, so I play some bossa nova music to help keep my focus on the road.

During this driving experience I decide to plan the next overseas holiday at the same time as enjoying the present moment. Mapping out which cities in Sweden, France and Italy to visit in sequence at first presents a challenge, until I stop thinking about it. By being patient, still, quiet and simply focusing on the road, the answers reveal themselves. Being able to engage in productive thought and simultaneously be present is a wonderful thing.

Well, that took about twenty minutes to set the holiday plan in place. And it is filed away in the mind's archive and forgotten about for now. My hands gently grip the steering wheel as I tilt my head slightly from side to side to avoid any stiffness on this long drive and start whistling a tune from Vivaldi's *Four Seasons* composition.

And now, being stuck in a traffic jam while driving to work is proving a great way to access the ever-patient consciousness. It is insightful to witness several cases of Fight/Flight responses among frustrated drivers. Some are beeping their horns, shouting and waving their arms outside the window, whilst others are trying to get off the road, drive across nature strips or perform dangerous U-turns to find an alternative route.

The rescuing side of my Being says it would be good right now to have a large sign saying, *Take three deep breaths in/out and smile,* and mount it on top of the car roof for motorists to see and act on the call to action. A few years ago that would have been me getting frustrated. And today I remain completely calm and capitalise on the opportunity to meditate with eyes open in a contemplative state.

And actually, it is an ideal time to reflect on what is important in life. I give rise to the realisation that this traffic jam and the frustration it is causing is a 'first world' problem. Also, the more I don't think about this situation, the quicker time passes. Cars move slowly along the road. Cyclists and motorbike riders cruise past all the stationary cars and even a couple of joggers plod by on the roadside. Just observing the surroundings in a non-judgemental way is proving to be entertaining enough.

And now, in my human form I sit in a comfortable chair that is moving at 60mph, surrounded by a metal frame on wheels with an engine. In front of the silence there is a faint whistling sound that vibrates gently in my ears. After observing momentarily the creases in my thumbs that grip the steering wheel, I look towards the road ahead. In my peripheral vision, a blur of pink cherry blossom trees rush past on both sides. I briefly contemplate the thought that life can also be a blur if one is living in a dream of the past and future and ignoring the present moment.

A long gap between thoughts is here now … and a warm feeling of inner peace and serenity engulfs me, followed by the realisation that the formlessness of consciousness is constant and lives within my physical human body and at the same time my physical human body is recycling through consciousness moment by moment. Regardless of where I am, how fast I travel on the ground, underwater, or flying in a plane in the sky, Presence exists.

In this moment, tingly sensations all over my body and a feeling of lightness overcome me as I experience the powerful sense of Presence. A blissful unity with all surroundings is ever present as I am awakened yet again to this spiritual being having a human experience.

And now, I turn off the highway onto the beaten track in country New South Wales towards the great town, Leeton – home to famous orange juice and rice manufacturing – to give a teaching session on shifting consciousness. Having never ventured this far to inland Australia before, most things are unfamiliar to me. I am experiencing a heightened sense of awareness and curiosity. With the wonderment of a child, I smile continually with my mouth half open in awe of the sunburnt flat landscaped countryside. Even if I wanted to, I could not put labels on some of the wildlife and nature that passes me by moment by moment. A mesmerising subtle wind sounds constantly. It is but the sky, clouds and trees with which I am familiar. For long stretches, the straight road seems to go on forever and ever; punctuated by interesting indigenous names of towns I cannot pronounce. After all, it is merely the sounds of vowels and syllables (silly-labels) that put the brand on certain communities of inhabitants.

I roll the window down, place my hand outside and feel the dry heat suck the coolness of air-conditioned oxygen from within the car. The earthy smells of the outback enter the vehicle and provide a pleasant woody aroma inside for the rest of the journey. This alerts me to the subtle deep spiritual nature that exists all around.

And now, for some fun and adrenaline, I sit inside a go-kart with my buttocks literally only five inches above the ground, alongside a few others in their karts waiting for final safety instructions before accelerating down the track. The course boasts a few obstacles and tight corners to negotiate. I lift my head to see what awaits me up ahead. Although my intention is just to have fun, a competitive entity that lives in the archives of my mind is likely to surface, present itself, and cause me to overtake anyone in my way. Ready, Set, Go!

My foot depresses the accelerator pedal and the zippy little go-kart takes off like a released elastic band. Approaching the first corner, there is nothing other than paying attention in this present moment or else I either crash or someone will overtake me. As I brake slightly and commence turning, centrifugal force pulls my body to the right as I resist. In the lead, my peripheral vision cannot see another go-kart alongside me. The tiny leather steering wheel is sensitive to every movement from left to right and it is taking a heightened sense of alertness to control the direction of the machine.

Being so low to the ground and travelling at such fast speeds creates the illusion of an even faster riding experience … The ride is finished now and the first thing I notice is how clear my head is, and new space existing within.

And now, there is no room for the wandering mind to distract me from these narrow winding roads going down a steep mountain. Fern trees are hanging over the edge; there are sudden hairpin turns appearing and not always safety railings on the roadside to protect cars from disappearing over the small cliff faces.

It intrigues me how the universe will place people in situations that make them present and alert to unfolding moments. Being attentive to cars coming towards me in the opposite direction is also consuming attention. Soft piano music pipes throughout the vehicle, adding another dimension of harmonic calmness and bliss to this lovely driving adventure.

A number of small dead furry animals on the road are being avoided by passing motorists, making it even more important to be attentive to the present moment. Off to the left side of a tight turn in the road is a tiny cave called Pooh's Corner. I smile as I see several species of stuffed toy bears congregating just inside the entrance. There is hardly enough space for one car to stop and observe the childlike display, so I merely slow down to take a glance before continuing on.

And now, cruising down the highway, I see a car coming the opposite way, flashing its lights. I sense this is to warn of a police car up ahead, monitoring car speeds. Checking my speedometer, I note it is within the set limit. A few moments pass by and out of the corner of my vision, I see red and blue lights followed by the sound of a piercing siren enter the road, having performed a rapid U-turn. Suddenly the police car is right behind me. The lights and sounds are blinding and deafening. The thought of being pulled over and charged for speeding does not cross my mind; a sense of alertness is ever so present as I wait for the policeman to overtake me. I decide to pull over to the side to let him pass. His car zooms past in a flash in pursuit of another motorist ahead.

I re-enter the highway feeling joyous for having remained calm during this short and frantic situation. There is much truth to the fact that being mindful and present to each and every moment will diffuse any thoughts, feelings or sensations related to unnecessary worry.

I marvel at the difference in reaction that may have occurred years ago in my less evolved state before developing my regular mindfulness and meditation practice. It could have resulted in sweaty palms, increased heart rate, and wild stories coming from voices in the head wondering why the police car is almost touching the bumper bar of my 'speed compliant' moving vehicle. Ah yes, yet another priceless benefit of living consciously and not identifying with the mind alone.

And now, the traffic in front of me has come to a grinding halt. Some time passes before the cars start moving slowly forward again. I drive past the scene of a three-car pile-up, where two of the vehicles have had their rear end smashed and dented. Pieces of glass and metal parts lie on the road. As I drive past the accident scene, I overhear one driver shouting at another: "If you were paying attention to the road and not looking at your phone, you would not have smashed up my arse!"

The guy making this statement has a fair point. In other words, if the reckless driver had been living in the present moment, alert and aware of the surroundings, the crash may have been avoided. Life is always teaching us lessons. As I reflect on the current situation, flashbacks pop into my mind of a few scenarios where I had momentarily drifted off in idle thought and lapsed in concentration, almost causing an accident myself.

For me, witnessing this accident scene is a wake-up call to stay focused on the road and surrounding cars at all times. I can tell that this has also been an awakening for the drivers in front of me, as their cars move deliberately slower than the speed limit for at least a while longer.

And now, observing the taxi driver taking me to the airport is an interesting experience. As he drives, taking the shortcuts to get me there quicker, I note that each time he puts his foot on the brakes, he coughs. I wonder if this is just a mild obsessive compulsive disorder, habit or a sore throat that needs clearing each time the car slows down.

The backseat smells like a brewery and yet there is a bowl of mouth-freshening mints sitting on the mid console for passengers to indulge in. A couple of tattered magazines protrude from the back of the front seat pockets. The driver is not speeding and is mindfully remaining within the set speed limit while whistling a tune foreign to me.

His mobile phone is ringing now and he chooses to answer it via an earpiece that is inserted in his left ear. Within moments another car beeps furiously at the taxi driver who is now distracted and hasn't noticed that the traffic lights have turned green. It is amazing to see in just a short twenty-minute taxi ride what can occur when someone mixes being mindful and mindless together. The shifts of rising above and below the canvas of the mind become obvious when observing others' behaviour.

Mindlessness

Being under the influence of alcohol and illicit drugs is a recipe for disaster on the road. Losing one's temper at another driver who is seemingly in the wrong is another example of mindlessness. And being distracted by loud music, eating with one hand and the other on the steering wheel, sending a text message, or turning around to look out the side or back window for a prolonged period of time is also putting one's self and others in danger.

Techniques to Apply

Take a slightly different route to the usual roads. This will encourage being present to a new driving experience. After you next finish driving or catching public transport, write down what you observed inside the vehicle, and how you responded to traffic and outside surroundings.

CHAPTER 7

EXERCISING

How Mindfulness Helps

If you are sensitive and alert on a continual basis to the way your body is moving from the breathing to the muscle movement, even the most repetitive exercises will become more interesting to perform. The Being in each present moment then becomes almost effortless. And as awareness broadens to take in surrounding sights, sounds, smells, tastes and touches while in motion, you may find yourself motivated to exercise a little longer or more intensely. Eventually you become tuned in to the subtleties of your connection between mind, body and soul. Once you can connect all the dots, you enter what many sports people refer to as 'the zone' – a place where synchronicity occurs and all goes according to plan.

The Diary

And now, walking briskly around the university campus proves to be refreshing, youthful and therapeutic. Each footstep crunches the gravel path beneath my feet. The sound of its rhythm keeps me present and the coolness of the intermittent breeze blowing against my skin is soothing. The smell of flowers and lake weeds drift from the water banks, and students passing by laugh in a carefree manner.

As sweat starts to emerge from my pores, I shed the light jacket. The extra coolness against my perspiring skin intensifies and I find my stride lengths increase with more mobility. The gap in between the last two thoughts was rather long. Human movement combined with a calm mind in the present moment equals bliss to me.

Gliding along, I really feel the Presence of unity consciousness. For moments at a time I am looking down upon my physical form body. I like the fact that I am here, there and everywhere. Flowing with this continuum of energy, I dance in this dimension with the sway of each tree branch, independent of time and space. In this moment back in my body, the next breath and the next footstep are all that really matters. Walking through the main university plaza now among many students melds my energy with others', giving a sense of abundant freedom and infinite possibility.

And now, just lying on the bed, performing core exercises starting with the simple movements of contracting and relaxing the perineum in a repetitive motion, works the internal lower abdominal muscles. Also, known in yoga as the core lock, I feel the benefits of stimulating this muscle group as a protective mechanism for the lower back with any sudden lifting movements. This exercise is similar to cutting off the flow of urine with this muscle group.

Also, by imprinting the small of my back into the bed mattress, I feel a bigger group of outer core abdominal muscles tense. I then exhale on the release. Repeating this motion several times gives me a sense of stability as if the spine is being hugged and secured.

The final step being conducted now is with hands behind my head and lifting my neck up to look at the toes. A group of core muscles further up the body is put through their paces. After fifty repetitions,

I feel a burning sensation in my upper abdominal muscle, as lactic acid struggles to be metabolised due to lack of oxygen there. So listening to the body, I cease the exercise, remain flat in a corpse pose and simply rest in the new energy flowing through my torso. Integrating the energy from all these body movements gives rise to a new harmonious vibration in every cell.

And now, sitting still in the car parked at the shopping centre, I commence exercising my eye muscles. Firstly I look up towards my eyebrow centre and hold this position for fifteen seconds. The next step is to look down at my nose tip for a similar timeframe, followed by glancing up towards the left and right sides of my head and down towards the left and right sides of my legs. With my hand now, I cover both eyes for thirty seconds just restfully looking into the semi darkness...

The eye muscles are feeling relaxed and I realise that this exercise being done on a regular occasion can indeed strengthen the vision and focus. I sense it is important to protect and look after the windows to the soul for as long as I am physically on this earth.

It is pleasing to reflect on the fact that forming a habit doing this simple exercise can eliminate the need for spending money on eyeglasses and the inconvenience of not being able to read small text in a critical situation. Even just after this short exercise, smaller text and items seem much clearer. It also feels as if I have had a head massage around the temple and forehead region. A few deep breaths in and out enhance my centred state of Being.

And now, slowly shuffling my feet, I put my best foot forward and break into a light jog. Immediately I become present to the physical body's aches and stiffness surrounding knee and hip joints, muscles and tendons. Eventually these sensations disappear as blood circulates throughout my human machine. A sense of joy starts to overwhelm me as I connect with surrounding nature and become aware of the nice feelings in my body thanks to the release of a chemical cocktail of dopamine, serotonin and other endorphins in my brain.

Within a few more minutes, I am in full stride and feel my feet leave the earth together every other moment, invoking a flying and floating sensation – airborne and suspended until the force of gravity grounds me again and again.

After ten miles, the mind and physical body remind me it will soon be time to stop running and rest. The mind is intervening with distress signals and for a short period, I slow down the pace and acknowledge the 'call to action'. Now the ego surfaces and tells me that once I ran twenty-six-mile marathons in less than three hours and should be able to push through pain barriers and run much faster than I am doing right now. Interestingly, when I pick up the pace again and start moving faster than before, a dose of adrenalin is released temporarily, numbing the pain and fatigue in true Fight or Flight fashion.

And now, I sit on a wooden bench in a park, surrounded by acres of green grass, mature willow trees and gravel pathways weaving their way in and around the park area. A faint sound of trickling water comes from a fountain hidden around the corner.

Butterflies flutter by and a gang of ducks make their way towards me, stopping within inches of my feet, curious at my state of being and perhaps hopeful for food to drop from my hand onto the ground below.

People are coming and going, some just lying still on a blanket, looking up at the sky, while others jog past or ride bicycles. It is almost two hours now that I have been sitting here simply looking, listening and closing my eyes, meditating. Observers may question that I am not doing any exercise and suggest it may benefit me to get up and go for a walk or move my body around a little. In fact I am exercising and resting my brain at the same time!

The alpha, gamma, theta and delta brainwaves making their way into the neural pathways headquarters of the lump of meat between my two ears are being felt to varying degrees. I guess one could call this a full brain workout of sorts.

And now, there is a free swim lane reserved for intermediate swimmers over there on the far side of the Olympic-size swimming pool. Placing the goggles over my head and around my eyes, I walk mindfully past the faster people gliding through the water. I take a few deeper breaths in and out while dangling my legs in the cool water. As soon as I submerge myself fully into the chilly water and start traversing down the lane in freestyle fashion, Presence intensifies.

The repetition of three arm strokes and a breath on alternate sides of each shoulder whilst staring at a black painted line on the pool floor, gives little opportunity for unnecessary thoughts to surface in the mind. Paying attention to only one stroke at a time and not trying to get to the other end of the pool, makes the experience of being buoyant and moving forward simultaneously peaceful and pleasurable.

The strong smell of chlorine subsides as the vibrating sound of each exhale creates the distraction and some kind of transcendence. The muscles, ligaments, tendons and joints start loosening up with each lap and now the mind, body and spirit are synchronising. There is renewed energy ever present and flowing from head to toe and back again.

And now, I am folding forward at the hips with feet firmly planted on the yoga mat, holding my elbows, softening the muscles in my neck and just letting go while I sway from side to side, limp like a ragdoll. There is an instant release of tension in my back. An awakening of a physical kind occurs as fresh, rejuvenating blood travels down towards my brain, giving an injection of youthfulness.

Releasing my elbows and sweeping my hands up towards the sky and reaching into the fingertips on the inhale helps to create freedom in the body by lengthening both sides. Bringing hands in prayer position to the heart centre on the next exhale, simultaneously grounding all four corners of the feet into the earth, returns me to home base before saluting the sun. Inhaling and raising the arms up parallel either side of the head, and swan diving down to the floor before planting the hands firmly into the mat and floating my legs to the back of the mat, sees me flow like water and soften like air.

From a high to low plank, my body lowers with gravity horizontal to the earth before scooping through with an arched back while gazing up towards the eyebrow centre. I now tuck my toes under and recline to a position with heels towards the back of the mat, buttocks in the air, fingers spread wide, with hands firmly planted whilst looking back towards the navel. I rest here for five breaths, feeling earthed and centred.

And now, my inner child is lit up with glee as the right foot strikes the footpath, propelling my form one more time as I regain balance on the skateboard. Cutting the air in motion, there is a gentle roar of four rubber wheels and ball bearings sounding below my feet. A ticklish vibration of Presence works its way up from my legs and into the hips and chest. The downhill slope appears over the horizon and gives a boost of momentum to the plank on wheels. An increase in alertness and attention is now required as the jolly whistling ceases, thoughts are dissolved into intense concentration, ensuring an accident does not occur.

There is a real sense of freedom and satisfaction making it in one piece to the bottom of the slope. My mind has been cleared and my head seems to have more space. Rolling to a stop, I pick up the board and feel the heat, vibration and energy in the black rubber wheels. I don't know if it is coming from my hands or the skateboard, however I trust that it does not really matter. It is what it is in this present moment. Just another sign that the universe has amazing ways of creating constant energy and multi-dimensional levels of consciousness.

And now, the mountain bike clicks over to a higher gear to negotiate the steepness of the rocky hill ahead. My buttocks rise up out of the seat to gain strength in the legs with each rotation of the pedals and crank shafts. A drop of salty sweat lands from my eyebrow into my right eye and a painful stinging sensation sets in. The blinding sunset adds another degree of challenge as I huff and puff, making my way up the slope. A gear change relieves the resistance momentarily. I can feel my heart pounding and lactic acid creeping into the quadricep leg muscles, initiating a burning sensation.

As long as I continue to be present to one breath at a time whilst maintaining the current momentum, I know there will be no need to jump off the bike and walk alongside it before reaching the summit. By channelling the breath into each area of tension, I find temporary relief for this next moment. Lifting my head up to look around at the mountains on the horizon and surrounding town below takes my attention away from the tyres stumbling over the rocks, and I almost have an accident with the handlebars briefly wobbling from side to side.

The summit is now within reach and the anticipation releases a burst of adrenalin to numb the pain in my muscles. And here I am, stationary, still, off the bike and rotating 360 degrees, standing upright while resting in Being.

And now, I sit here doing push-ups for my brain. It may seem counter intuitive that stillness with eyes closed in a state of Being is actually great exercise for that organ of grey matter that floats under the skull. Yet it feels relaxing and calm to rest here knowing the goodness I am doing for myself. The breath is shallow and slow. A faint pulse rate ticks over as I bring my attention to the heart centre.

A glowing golden light gradually appears at my eyebrow centre and starts pulsating as my brain produces gamma waves. As it does, I step up its exercises to a new pace. A warm, tingling sensation cascades down my spine towards the feet. Wow, it's no wonder that more and more people are waking up to this kind of workout nowadays. It feels so good and brings about a deeper sense of peace and tranquillity.

The mind is persistent with attempts to distract this exercise. It is saying things like, "That meeting starts in thirty minutes from now", "You forgot to take your multivitamin before you left the house" and, "Which route will I jog today?" So I gently open my eyes and fix a soft gaze towards the nose tip to dissolve the thoughts and tame the wild elephant.

Mindlessness

I used to want to simply 'tick the box' each time I did some exercise because studies showed that it was good for me and minimised risks of chronic illness like heart disease, diabetes, cancer, obesity and Alzheimer's. However, this actually led to a lack of motivation. Eventually my mind convinced me it was so hard to get out of the chair or bed that I would let weeks and months go by without moving my body at all. I found that being mindless almost all the time led to a downward spiral, which ended up on the path to deterioration of the mind and body.

Techniques to Apply

Perform your exercise of choice paying attention to every movement whilst being aware of what is happening in your mind and body. Find some fun in the body movement activity you choose. Participate in a team sport or in an exercise routine with a friend or loved one. Journal your findings of the experience.

CHAPTER 8

SLEEPING & DREAMING

How Mindfulness Helps

By being mindful with a single point focus on dropping into both the first two states of consciousness – 1) deep sleep and 2) dreaming – one allows oneself the best chance of the body and mind being fully rested and rejuvenated from the waking state of consciousness and all its challenges encountered. In the present moment before closing the eyes, the mind will ultimately be in a 'no thought' mode of peace and serenity. Then, entering the sleep and dream states can occur quickly. A brain that is accustomed to an ongoing mindfulness practice is bound to experience deeper sleep and more pleasant dreams.

The Diary

And now, I have woken up from a dreaming state with a smile on my face and in my heart. What is fascinating to me is how vivid the dream was – colours, sights, sounds, motions, connections with people…

I recall I was in line behind several people approaching a spiritual teacher at the front of a room. The faceless, androgynous teacher, was asking each person in a deep voice, "Who are you?" When the question was answered in a particular way, a gift was handed to each one. I could not hear answers to the questions being posed until I was only behind a couple of people before the teacher. It seemed curious that more people were not receiving a gift.

Then it struck me that the people not receiving a gift and returning to the back of the line were answering the question with descriptions related to name, age, nationality, body weight, height and other labels or statuses. When it came to my turn to answer the question, I replied with great joy:

"I am consciousness expressing itself through a human being."

A gift was handed to me. When I took it, a deep feeling of unity infused my Being. I sit here now consciously with eyes open, reflecting on the meaning behind the wonderful, enlightening dream.

And now, everywhere I go to get away from the person chasing after me, that person keeps appearing within seconds of my arrival at the next destination. Even when I leap from building to building, tumbling down many flights of stairs and swimming for long distances underwater to escape, that being appears again and again within moments of me surfacing. It is exhausting always being on the run like this, and I wish I could be still and catch my breath for at least a few minutes before moving on again. It becomes apparent that I am actually somewhere in the Chicago region of the United States of America.

All of a sudden my eldest cousin's face crystalizes in front of me, revealing it is she who is chasing me around wherever I go. She shouts to me as I flee again, "I just want to talk to you about the family reunion next year!"

Relieved that my pursuer means me no harm, I breathe out a big sigh, smile and wake from this bizarre dream to the sound of my phone buzzing a message alert. Whilst still feeling a strong sense of my cousin's Presence, I get out of bed to check the phone message. In total delight and bemusement I discover it is cousin Christy in the USA, whom I haven't spoken to for many years, who is communicating in real time on Facebook Messenger about the upcoming family reunion. It is fascinating to read her sequence of messages, which include questions for my input, relating directly to the dream from which I have just awoken.

And now, suddenly I wake up in a lather of sweat, gasping for breath from a dream that involved me as a victim of a European terrorist attack about to unfold. Someone was running towards me in a crowd with a bomb strapped to his waist just as thousands of us were about to commence running an organised marathon.

I wrestled to escape the dense pack of people, yelling out that there was a man approaching with an explosive device. Few runners paid attention to me and most just let me run past. I ran as fast as I could without turning back, expecting to hear a loud explosion, but it never happened.

Without overanalysing the dream, it quickly becomes apparent to me that a recent terrorist attack in downtown Sydney, plus the fact that I have been injured physically on a number of occasions over the last few months, may be responsible for the experience from which I just woke up. As the breath and heart rate re-establish their natural patterns, the ever-reliable present moment is noticeable again and begins to absorb all remaining sensations, images, feelings and thoughts related to the dream. A wave of gratitude and humility washes through me as I sit up in bed, reflecting on my fortune to live in a relatively free country of conscious people.

And now, I wake up feeling a chill travelling up my spine and am present to a lightness of Being like nothing ever experienced before. Before opening my eyes, I recall that during my dream I was flying off the floor within the confines of the house somewhere. As moments pass by here in bed, I recollect vividly standing in the corner of a large room with no furniture and feeling my feet leave contact with the ground as I levitated up towards the high ceiling in an upright vertical position. At first my initial instinct was to resist and try descending to reconnect with the earth, but quickly I started enjoying the floating experience. With a simple glance in a certain direction, I would be directed to that location whilst being suspended in the air, slowly travelling to the next part of the room.

Feeling playful, I started moving in all directions. The song 'And She Was' performed by music band Talking Heads was playing in the background. The experience was so much fun. And as I began to open my eyes and take a few deeper breaths in, in this super dream state, I also performed several somersaults mid-air, followed by pushing myself off each wall with my feet.

This magical anti-gravity experience has me in a state of wonder about other dimensions of Being. I trust that this loving, ethereal and playful dimension will occur again in another dream.

And now, after my attention starts drifting and my eyes start closing, I am brought back into the present moment when I hear Annika say: "Dad, have you been lucid dreaming before?"

Astonished and impressed with her deep question relating to a level of consciousness, I reply: "Have you?"

"Not yet, but I am planning to do it," responds this creative youngster who operates at a higher state of consciousness than most.

With a heightened sense of Presence, I listen attentively to her description of lucid dreaming:

"You see, Dad, it happens when you keep a journal of all your dreams by writing them down as soon as you wake up, before you have a chance to forget about them. Then just before you go to sleep at night, you look at the dream list and decide which one you want to revisit."

In silence, I remain in awe at Annika's state of Being and feel a unique sense of inspiration and insight. When she realises I'd like to discuss this topic further, she quickly changes the subject. The conversation now moves away from lucid dreaming to inviting her girlfriends over for a party.

And now, lying down on a bed with my head on the pillow, I bring my attention to the rise and fall of my chest and stomach with each inhale and exhale of breath. Acknowledging the coolness of air through the nostrils with each breath in and the warmth of the outgoing breath exiting the body, I allow my eyelids to gently close, settling into a deeper state of rest. My body softens as I scan past the neck, shoulders, arms, torso, hips, legs and feet.

There is a sense of warmth and comfort as I drop deeper and deeper and deeper into the depths of restfulness. The gaps between each thought are getting longer and the thoughts blurrier as the mind is at complete ease and the breath becomes less frequent and more shallow … a sense of stillness continues to wash over and inside me, luring me into a state of Stage 1 sleep. Completely melting all the body parts into the mattress, tranquillity and peace ripple through me.

Allowing myself to completely let go of the senses – sight, sound, smell, touch, taste – I count down from 10, 9, 8, 7, 6, 5, 4, 3, 2, 1 and slip into sleeping mode.

And now, knowing that enough sleep is one of the four pillars for healthy living and longevity, I take a short nap aboard an aircraft bound for Adelaide, Australia. With my seatbelt loosened slightly around my waist, I exhale deeply and surrender to the soft, comfortable passenger seat, allowing my physical body to mould into the contours of the chair. The gentle hum of the plane's engine muffles the thoughts in my mind and helps the brain to arrive at a very restful position.

All the five senses take a break, the body totally relaxing and zzzzzzzzzz…

I regain consciousness to the soft voice over the speakerphone: "We are commencing our descent so please place your chairs in an upright position and fasten your seatbelts."

Sleep is literally priceless. I rest in awareness for several moments in a semi-conscious state with my eyelids half open. There is a sense of alertness and I feel all my cells recharging with more energy. It is wonderful to recognise and cherish those moments of rejuvenation when sleep is available to take place and that it does not necessarily have to be in a bed between 10pm and 6am.

Having a regular meditation practice makes it easier to still the mind and relax the body on a consistent basis in order to enabling dozing off.

And now, sitting up in bed, I peel my eyelids open to see the alarm clock tick over to 4am. What instantly becomes fascinating to me is that since I first closed my eyes to sleep at 10pm, I have not lost consciousness and slipped into the normal unconscious state where all five senses are temporarily suspended.

Yes, the mind is faintly participating in the experience, commenting every now and then on how I have been able to accomplish staying still in this position for approximately six hours with limited movement in my form body. I have been in a meditative state of Being for longer than I can remember. Not feeling so tired, I reclose my eyelids and delve into the depths of inner space for a while ... and when I reopen my eyes, the clock says 6:35am and daylight peeps in through the curtains and onto the cupboard at the end of the bed.

I am unsure whether I actually fell asleep or not. It does feel refreshing to pull myself out of bed, though.

There appears to be no physical or mental fatigue as I go about my daily routine. My conclusion is that I simply rested in consciousness for several hours with very little intervention from my mind; something that quite easily could have expressed frustration, resulting in exhaustion in this moment.

And now, driving down the highway, my eyelids start to get heavy as fatigue sets in. I find an appropriate place on the side of the road to pull over, park and have a power nap. The seat is reclined; I settle into a restful position and reconnect with my breath. The sound of passing vehicles on the highway in between the faint whistle of the inhale and exhales take me into a shallow sleep. The muffled sound of the cicadas orchestra in the arid bushland outside disappear ... 7:15pm the clock says after I regain consciousness and open my eyes to the semi-darkness of dusk. Feeling recharged after only fifteen minutes of light sleep, I proceed to pull the driver's seat into its original position, secure the seatbelt, turn on the indicator and check in the rear view mirror before gently compressing the foot pedal, accelerating and re-entering the highway to continue the journey home.

I reflect on the benefits of a quick nap and feel a sense of new energy travelling all throughout my body. The head feels spacious and peaceful, the hands and feet strong and the natural breath is deeper and less frequent. The mind is still and resting for a while.

And now, I am woken out of a deep slumber to the soft sound of THUMP, THUMP, THUMP under the bed. Immediately I recognise it is Stella, who has snuck into the bedroom during the night and fallen asleep. In a semi-conscious state, I continue to hear the rhythmic thumping of her tail against the carpeted floor as I glance across at the clock to see the time of 3:31am.

Growing more curious, I lean over the edge of the bed and shine a penlight torch on the white fluffy dog who is sound asleep, eyes closed, tongue hanging out with an actively wagging tail. I conclude that she must be having a nice dream. After all, dogs also recycle their form bodies through consciousness. It is cute to hear Stella start whimpering happily as if anticipating food, before her front paw starts scratching her tummy. My mind intervenes again and assumes that she must be experiencing an amazing dream.

So rather than intervene by waking her up and asking her to leave the bedroom, I decide to let sleeping dogs lie, while I rest still on my back with eyes closed, patiently waiting for the tail-thumping to stop so I can drift back into an unconscious state myself.

Mindlessness

In a previous time in life, I believed that to have a good sleep it was acceptable to drink a bottle of wine and take two strong headache tablets before my head hit the pillow. A TV show of any kind being viewed while lying in bed would provide further mental anaesthetic to fast track the sleeping process. And because I was worried about having nightmares rather than nice dreams, I hoped each night before I closed my eyes that I would not enter a dream state at all until I regained consciousness several hours later the next morning.

Techniques to Apply

Limit or eliminate alcohol at least two hours before sleep time. Write on a piece of paper what you would like to dream about that night and put it under your pillow. Drink a small glass of warm milk, honey and cinnamon before bedtime. Turn all electronic devices off prior to resting your head on the pillow. Whilst reviewing the events of the day just passed, take ten deeper breaths and on the exhale visualising all the day's events dissolving. Get comfortable, close your eyes and go to sleep. Surrender and be open to anything in the sleep and dream states of consciousness.

CHAPTER 9

FEELING

How Mindfulness Helps

Adopting a mindfulness practice and befriending yourself will lead you to enhanced emotions within your being and compassion for others around you. Feelings of deep joy, peace, calm and euphoria can be cultivated by paying attention to the present moment regularly enough. Everyone is different and evolves at their own pace. And being consistent with the practice of mindfulness gradually changes what you may once have not been sensitive to or considered important to feel. An evolution of feeling more and thinking less transpires over time and is so subtle that one day it may suddenly dawn on you that a major transformation has taken place by way of an awakening. It could be that the shift in consciousness had been there for a while, however until you got out of your own way of the busy mind, it was not yet apparent.

The Diary

And now, I reach for the remote control and turn on the television, knowing that nothing has changed in the way world events are portrayed to the public on the free to air channels. Sure enough, the first images are graphic scenes of people being shot dead in another country for no apparent reason. I am left feeling sadness for the innocent victims and their families. The next news clip is about a company that has terminated the employment of staff members in a downsizing exercise. The footage shows people looking devastated as they leave their building with boxes of belongings in hand.

Yes, in many cases misery loves company, however this evening I am opting out of unnecessary negative feelings. I am grateful in this moment that through many meditation sessions and a regular mindfulness practice, I feel compassion for those affected by atrocities through no fault of their own. As I switch off the television, I can comfortably say that I won't be checking in again on the news for a very long time to come.

In this present moment, there exists a regathering of peace, acceptance and gratitude for life as it is and recognition of the unconsciousness existing on our planet earth.

And now, while Annika orders her chocolate milkshake and donut with cinnamon dust and sugar frosting from the sales assistant at Donut King, I feel a peaceful sense of Presence overcoming me while observing the franchise storeowner. The ever-present owner is carefully and deliberately lifting the glass lid that covers the colourful donut selection to place special promotional Christmas stickers on display.

With a permanent smile on his face and the gentle humming of 'Jingle Bells' escaping his lips, this elderly gentleman is spreading vibes of love and joy all around him. Whilst waiting to be served, I observe other patrons also delighting in the Donut King man as he mindfully goes about his business, spreading Christmas cheer. For some reason, one person frowns and shakes his head as though in disapproval. I don't know why, but that's okay.

The insight I am gaining from the storeowner is that he is approaching the winter of his life and appears physically frail. And yet there is a glow of consciousness that radiates from the inside out, just like a lantern. His light seems to touch those within a certain radius as he manoeuvres his way around the front of his shop counter, still whistling. There is a change in tune as the Christmas medley switches to 'Winter Wonderland'.

And now, Stella senses I am going for a walk. She observes the pair of running shoes I select from the cupboard. Her tail starts wagging frantically, causing her body to sway from side to side. Dogs are certainly always in the present moment. As soon as my laces are tied, she heads straight to the front door and sits patiently in front of it. I reach for her lead hanging behind the cupboard, clip it on her collar and proceed to walk her into the bushland dominated by gumtrees, fire trails and roaming wild kangaroos.

As we approach a bunch of these adorably strange marsupials, Stella tries to sprint towards them only to forget she is chained to a lead that chokes her momentarily. And with mixed feelings, something tells me she needs to be set free to satisfy her curiosity about these hopping furry animals. I let her off the lead and witness all but one large male kangaroo take flight and jump away, disappearing into the bushes.

As Stella chases the pack of roos, she suddenly stops and notices one giant marsupial, standing tall and upright while balancing on its tail and hind legs with its chest puffed out, ready for battle. Stella skids to a grinding halt and starts barking at the kangaroo. Without consideration for the dog's feelings, the giant marsupial tries to kick her, causing her to switch from Fight to Flight mode. She runs back to me, whimpering, with her tail between her legs.

And now, I am feeling an expanding awareness and spaciousness from the inside out. It is challenging to write about because no words in any language can effectively describe the sense of Being in this moment. It seems that humanity at large is my community and the planet earth is a backyard in which I can play. As I continue to drop lingering stories in my head, feelings of deeper joy surface in consciousness and my smile widens and becomes more permanent. And as I put aside my old belief systems and concern for looking good, I become at peace with wearing comfortable clothes rather than matching colours and popular brand labels.

There are no longer feelings of sadness for how my life once was. Instead I cry tears of joy at the sheer beauty of life itself and for the unnecessary suffering caused by human unconsciousness to innocent beings. And since I have understood and agreed that one can never manage time, I am not as frantic anymore 'doing' and instead, enjoying more 'being' whilst still accomplishing what is essential on a daily basis, moment by moment.

Feeling an energy continually passing through my physical body now is beautiful and almost ticklish. It is as if each and every cell is being massaged with a feather. How wonderful!

And now, being present to a fundamental exercise of feeling subtle energy in my hands and feet, grounds and centres me immediately but not abruptly. It is amazing to note that by just being aware of all the fingers and toes, an energy becomes noticeable. It is always there and often goes unnoticed due to other distractions. From this point onwards, it is amusing to visualise the spreading of this energy as it travels into the hands, wrists, foot arches and up the legs and down the arms.

And actually, I am alert to the fact that the energy is constantly there throughout the whole body, however it is only apparent when the attention is directed towards it. This exercise is causing the breath to become less frequent and more regular. The gaps in between thoughts are also getting longer. A couple of ideas are bubbling up to the mind's surface. I am content to be in this state of Being for a longer period. The pulse rate in my physical body has slowed down considerably and yet there is an alertness in the current Isness that exists.

Now I can feel this same subtle energy expanding up through my head, down the back of the neck and all the way back to the feet. Engulfed in this energy, I decide to get up and give my youngest son a hug to transfer the goodness to him.

And now, waiting in a long queue at the local café during the mid-morning rush for a cup of coffee, I become present to the feeling of gratitude. By looking and listening, I am able to observe many impatient, highly-strung, jittery humans wanting their caffeine fix *now*; I am grateful not to be affected by the tension existing around me. In fact, I am able to let this tension pass right through me, without any uneasy sensations arising. A woman behind me notes it is better to remain calm amongst this morning's mental chaos. She comments that patience is a virtue.

I smile and remark to the woman in front of me that the coffee will taste even better for having to wait this long. The barista behind the counter is synchronised with his team and producing several cups per minute for the anxious customers. He is calm and knows what to expect every morning at this time. The aromatic smell of the beans each time the coffee machine grinds them wafts through the café and causes a Mexican wave of nostrils flaring on the inhale breath of this beautiful aroma.

Hearing the waitress telling someone nearby that the café makes in excess of seven hundred cups of coffee each day, leaves me in a wondrous and contemplative state at the teamwork, mindfulness and continual alertness that is occurring moment by moment during this peak production period. Cup in hand now, I feel the warmth, smell the aroma, see the dark colour, hear the froth and taste the coffee.

And now, sitting quietly on a balcony overlooking the city with mountains in the background, I am overcome with a feeling of deep gratitude towards life in general. No particular aspects arise, nor are labels placed on this beautiful feeling. Euphoric sensations of vibration tingle throughout my physical body as I rest in Being. The total comfort that exists in my human form is indescribable. Words would merely veil this experience. *Thank you, God; thank you, God; thank you, God* is my mantra here and now.

A transformation and paradigm shift is occurring whereby I realise that we are all part of the universe; I am so very appreciative to be alive in this day and age where science and spirituality are coming together. And I am also feeling blessed to be in a position to teach people all over the world about a way of living with lightness through the power of shifting consciousness and experiencing new dimensions.

As I close my eyes gently now, the light of awareness pulsates in between the eyebrow centre, generating a vibrational warmth of deep blue colours. And in this present moment, time and space become irrelevant as Divine Consciousness sets in and all surroundings fuse into one experience.

And now, standing in the shower cubicle, half asleep, I turn on the faucet. As the fountain lands on my head and the temperature rises, I awaken fully with a sharp alertness. With the regulation of temperature to a comfortable warmth, I enjoy the micro massaging sensation of all the droplets caressing my skin. The soap is smooth and slippery, as I glide the bar up and down my torso, limbs and around my face. The steam fogs up the glass shower walls and in an opaque fashion, blurring the sight of everything on the other side.

My mind wanders, transporting me momentarily to a tropical rainforest, where tall, bright green plants and wildlife surround me. I take a deeper breath in and out and bring myself back to the present moment right here in the shower. I look down and observe my feet partially blocking the water from the holes in the drain cover. A puddle forms and starts expanding below.

It is now time to rinse my body in cold water. So I turn off the hot tap, crank up the cold water and gasp for air as my body awakens with the feeling of aliveness. The cold droplets contract and seal the many pores in my skin. Yes. This is when I know I am Presence.

And now, I am feeling acutely aware of many levels of consciousness simultaneously. In this moment of stillness, I recognise different dimensions of Being. I acknowledge my existing unconsciousness and observe my exact point of awareness. As I take the next breath in, I become alert to the five senses of sight, smell, sound, taste and touch. As I look at the distance between the trees outside the window and myself, I am aware of the space and subtle energy existing between us and the potential weight and density of the trees. In this dimension, time and space and the theory of cause and effect are ever present.

And whilst remaining aware of this present moment sitting here, fleeting images of the past and thoughts of the future arise in my mind. And in this multidimensional state, I feel that I am over there among the trees as well as right here, sitting in the chair.

I am Presence passing through this human body God has given me on this earth for a while. I feel very loving at the moment. The acknowledgement that I have a personal sense of identity inside the unity of everything, and the experience of all the vibrations coming together as one, are truly blissful.

Mindlessness

For so long I was comfortably numb, living under the canvas of the mind, too afraid to have feelings for myself or other people for fear of appearing weak, vulnerable and emotional. I made sure I was either really busy, busy, busy doing many things at once, or in a haze under the influence of alcohol or marijuana, so I was not at risk of feeling. And I was also constantly on the lookout for a fight or argument. When reflecting on this, I realise that I *was* actually feeling. It just so happens they were destructive feelings of anger, resentment, jealousy and hatred. Over time this kind of mindlessness hurt the health of my physical body and other human beings and living creatures around me.

Techniques to Apply

Before passing judgement on a situation, put yourself in the shoes of the other person and imagine how he or she would feel in that moment. Each time notable feelings arise, without judgement, jot down what is happening to you at the time. Witness and reflect on your journal notes without too much thought and accept what came up at that moment.

CHAPTER 10

PLAYING & LAUGHING

How Mindfulness Helps

When one is in a mindful state, a lightness of being permeates the soul, the wonderment of a child surfaces and humour can appear in the most unexpected situations. Because one becomes less worried about what others think, there is a tendency to be uninhibited and follow the heart's desires and not the logic of the mind. In many cases, playing leads to laughter and laughter leads to 'feel good' hormones being released in the brain, giving a sense of euphoria, calm and relaxation. Most children live in the 'now' and demonstrate to adults that it is playing and laughing that actually teach us about life and its machinations. Mindfulness helps us to look on the bright side of life.

The Diary

And now, it starts with a chuckle as I overhear the woman in the corner cackling. It just keeps going on and on and on. I start laughing to myself and it rapidly turns into a belly laugh. At first I try to control it by remaining silent so as to not draw attention to patrons dining in the café. I observe that is the ego rearing its ugly head, so I now evolve my laughter with an uninhibited sense of freedom, quickly erupting into a bellow of deep sound escaping my mouth. And in true contagious nature, several other people also start laughing with varying degrees of intensity. What is so beautiful is that all of us are unaware of the origin of our shared joy, except the woman in the corner who started it a few minutes ago.

And now, I observe several people who do not see the funny side of this current state of being. My mind starts making up a few stories as to why this is the case – "Maybe they are just angry with life," or, "They don't like seeing other people openly happy in public," or, "You are not supposed to behave inappropriately like this in public". Well, really only they know why they are not laughing or smiling at this moment.

So instead, I close my eyes for a few seconds and compassionately send the 'non laughers' some good vibrations.

And now, the comedy adventure film, *The Hangover*, has me in an uncontrollable fit of laughter. The slapstick comedy of error about three bachelors having a wild time before one of them gets married and its unimaginable, outrageous sequence of events brings me to a heightened sense of Presence. I pause in stillness for a few moments and feel a field of electricity travelling through me from head to toe.

Presence is now shifting from attention to the colourful character actors to the nice, aching sensations in my cheeks and abdominal muscles. Tears of joy are rolling down my face and I do not seem to be able to stop laughing. Feeling exhausted and out of breath, there is a timely resting point in the movie that allows me to recover from the laughing fit. Then, just like a big ocean wave, another punchline is delivered to the shore and laughter erupts inside again, causing another flood of 'feel good' healing and rejuvenating chemicals into my brain.

In a hilarious state of Being, I decide to turn the television off and rest in this most incredible feeling of euphoria and alertness. The goodness of this 'laughfest' is still tickling my soul and soothing the body from the crown of my head through to the tips of my toes. I know that my internal pharmacy has just poured a selection of the best natural chemicals into every cell that makes up my 'form-self'.

And now, while cooking dinner in the kitchen, I hear an explosion of laughter coming from the yoga studio next door. Curiously, I check the yoga class calendar and see that Sergei is teaching a specific session on 'laughter meditation' this evening.

This time an even louder explosion from many other students bellows and vibrates. And yes, contagiously I start chuckling to myself. On the next wave of hysterical laughing that seeps under the doorway and after a short moment to draw new breath, I burst out into chuckle after chuckle after chuckle, dropping the cooking utensils on the bench to wipe the tears of joy from my eyes. This is such a great feeling. Endorphins are flooding my brain by now and I decide to go peer through the door crack to see several people rolling around on mats in hysterics, holding their bellies and massaging the cramped cheeks of their faces.

I head back into the kitchen to resume cooking. Before I pick up the wooden spoon to stir the vegetables, I take a few moments to stand in stillness and feel an incredible sense of Presence touch my heart and every cell in my physical body. It feels like a million tiny feathers are tickling me inside.

And now, Oscar and I share a pinball machine game in an arcade. On each side of the machine we command the buttons that control the flippers responsible for sending the steel ball rolling back up and into the spring-loaded maze, with lights and electronic sounds that earn the player accumulating points on contact.

A variety of sounds in erratic rhythms are projected in coordination with a colourful display of lights. Numbers on the scoreboard tick over as we both smile at each other. Without words, we feel and sense oneness, love and joy that our father/son afternoon is going well.

I feel a buzzing vibration in my jeans from the mobile phone that could very well activate the distracting mind to attempt luring me away from the present moment. Choosing to ignore it, I refill the pinball machine with more coins. We continue our togetherness in harmony, enjoying each other's company immensely.

I am learning a lot from this beautiful young being as he lives in the present moment, uninhibited by thought distractions of the past or future. Periodically I glance across to watch his eyes follow every movement of the steel ball bouncing from side to side, travelling all over the machine. Marvelling at his attentiveness, I let the ball past my flipper and down the chute.

Oscar looks at me, frowning with disappointment and says, "Dad, you weren't paying attention!"

I smile and tell him that it's just a game.

And now, I am playing 'fetch' with Stella. Wow, talk about being in the present moment! Canines are naturally alert, aware and paying attention to every movement as if time does not exist. Hmm, I am learning a valuable lesson from my furry white four-legged friend. As I throw the rubber ball into the bushes in the backyard, Stella bounds fearlessly, throwing herself into the shrubs and quickly retrieving it.

She comes back to me and drops the slimy ball at my feet with enthusiasm. My eyes lock with hers and a heightened sense of Presence arises within. Distracted by a butterfly fluttering by, I feel Stella's paw tap my foot, suggesting that she detects I am no longer paying attention to her right now.

The game continues for a while longer until I hear my daughter calling me to help her with homework. As I leave the backyard to enter the house, Stella quickly drops the ball at my feet and sits between the house entrance and me. My mind tells me I need to rush in to help Annika; consciousness says to keep playing ball with Stella. I have a few more throws with the dog before anticipating a second cry for help from Annika.

Now everyone is satisfied. Homework supervision is taking place, the dog is happy and I feel a nice balance of energy among all.

And now, my two-year-old nephew is standing on a chair next to the recently decorated Christmas lunch table. Twenty guests are about to arrive just as Brandon decides to start playing with the decorations in the middle of the table. This most 'present moment' child curiously picks up shiny cutlery and rotates the spoon in his hand until the distorted reflection of his face catches his eye. In amusement, Brandon starts laughing at himself and the reflection. This alert and experimental youngster then decides to rearrange the glasses and napkins before attempting to pull apart the poppers to make a loud bang.

Deciding not to spoil the toddler's fun by alerting his mother or father to his playful, adventurous spirit, I continue to be amused by his every movement. Barbecue-flavoured crackers are being lifted by the fistful and placed into Brandon's mouth. There is a momentary delay as he stands still, acknowledging the savoury flavours on his tongue before breaking into a dance and stamping his feet on the floor and swinging his arms around his body while humming a tune to no apparent music. Now he starts marching up and down like a soldier, moving his head from side to side, blissfully enjoying the crackers being munched on. Vicariously, I live through Brandon's eyes just a few more precious moments.

And now, Oscar gives me a novelty toy of purple slime the size of a tennis ball for Christmas. I take it out of its plastic toy container. The sense of Presence arises quickly and thoughts dissolve as I start caressing this strange, gooey, cold, slimy substance in the palm of my hand and squishing it between my fingers. The texture is smooth and the shades of purple vary with each squeeze of the substance in the palm of my hand and between my fingers.

It does not appear to smell like anything at all. I throw the purple slime ball onto the window and it sticks momentarily before reluctantly sliding down the glass and eventually making contact with the floor. My inner child lights up as I take the slime ball toy and place it against my cheek. Another strange sensation of coolness overcomes me.

Pulling the substance apart proves fascinating as it becomes translucent when stretched open. This is a simple exercise in mindfulness – observing and experiencing the substance as it is and as it isn't, moulding it to the contours in the palms, feeling the soft texture and temperature against the skin whilst enjoying the gap of consciousness between each thought.

And now, as I open the motel front door to go outside to the car and get my glasses, a black and white kelpie dog appears at my feet with a worn out tennis ball in his mouth whilst gazing up into my eyes. There is an immediate resonance and connection between the two of us. Now, happily side-tracked, I start playing fetch with this sleek and super alert canine by throwing the ball several times as far away as I can down the steep grassy slope.

What is fascinating and insightful is how he locks his piercing blue-eyed gaze to mine as I contemplate the next place to chuck the ball. Intuitively the kelpie seems to know when I am trying to fool him with a fake throw and a real throw. Each time he delivers the ball back to my feet and then quickly backs up, crouching down, waiting patiently for the next move. This appears to be 100% dedication and attention to each moment and a much-loved activity. I am learning a lot from this active animal.

Eventually I cease the ball game after several throws to proceed to the car as originally planned. Upon opening the door to reach in for the glasses, I hear a faint sound of the tennis ball bounce towards my feet. As I look down to the ground, there is the dog again, seated. This time he places both front paws on my knees and looks up into my eyes with a slight tilt of the head, sad face and pointed ears pleading for the ball game to continue.

And now, I am playing the classical orchestral piece, 'Peter and The Wolf' by Sergey Prokofiev, on the stereo. Sitting in a comfortable position, gazing out the window into the forest, I start remembering the different story characters associated with the varying instruments. For example, the wolf is represented by the French horn, the duck is the oboe, Peter is represented by the string instruments, the flute for the bird, clarinet for the cat and bassoon for Grandpa.

What I become present to in this moment are vivid memories of the classroom, student and teachers during music lessons in Paris over forty years ago when I first learned this composition and its association between people, animals and musical instruments. Now I start marvelling at the mysterious nature of the brain and its ability to somehow store these crystal clear memories. To be distracted by the wandering mind while listening to this musical story would risk missing a crucial part of the plot.

I am amused as I see myself as a young child in fear of the wolf whenever the French horn sounds and relieved when I hear the happy string instruments of the naïve and confident Peter. Listening to the musical piece now, without the childhood flashbacks, brings me to a less imaginative position in the story and more of an appreciation of the assorted harmonic tones of the brass, woodwind, strings and percussion instruments. How fascinating to identify between child and adult perceptions of the same musical piece at different times in life.

And now, sitting next to a fellow yoga teacher friend and her playful baby, I notice the infant looking straight into my eyes. A connection is made between us and I smile in response. He smiles back, immediately exposing his toothless gums. We start communicating with each other independent of words. For the next couple of minutes, pure body language and limbic resonance take the two of us on a journey of discovery. The mother feels her baby's joy and starts giggling. Baby Sebastian acknowledges his mother's happiness and giggles too. I reach out towards Sebastian's hand with my finger. He clasps it with a strong grip and tries to place it in his mouth for the taste test.

I gently pull my finger away as he looks at me in wide-eyed astonishment. I mirror his look and widen my eyes too. Baby smiles. I lift my left eyebrow a few times and he makes an effort to mimic my movement. Sebastian now gurgles as he stares deep into the windows of my soul. So in true 'call and response' fashion, I do the same.

The pleasure of bringing out my inner child in this moment is beyond words. This is yet another proof point that simple and good hearted communication and connection can occur without the veil of language and words, regardless of biological age and development.

Mindlessness

Taking life too seriously and subscribing to the old-fashioned belief system that as an adult one must be conservative, not laugh too much or out loud, avoid childish games or being childlike, are representations of mindlessness. By also not paying attention to the game being played and being mentally absent, the delight of the moment is lost in an instant and can never be retrieved. And when laughter is forced and inauthentic, it too represents mindlessness and living in a moment other than the present.

Techniques to Apply

Find a few minutes each day to laugh and play. Recall fun games that as a child made you feel good and relive them. You may consider putting on music from your younger days during your playful moments. During downtime from work, download an episode of a funny TV show or movie that had you rolling around laughing and play it again. If you have a pet animal, spend more time playing with it. Consider investing in a pet if you don't already have one.

CHAPTER 11

TRAVELLING

How Mindfulness Helps

Whatever your definition of travel is, consciousness is the common denominator. And wherever you go, in whatever mode of transport you choose, at any speed, there you are! In other words, acknowledge and accept that your body and mind are travelling through consciousness simultaneously. Being mindful of this amazing fact can enhance your travel experience and take it to a new dimension. You may find yourself less bored on long flights, train and bus rides or car trips by marvelling at what is unfolding in each and every present moment on the journey. A mindfulness practice encourages the wonderment of a child to surface and truly appreciate the travelling experience.

The Diary

And now, as the airplane accelerates down the runway, I hear the deep rumble of engines gradually elevate their pitch into a crescendo. The feeling of the chair gently vibrating against my body subsides as the aircraft disconnects with the earth and I sink back into gravity. Opening my eyes to peer outside the window reveals a landscape below, becoming smaller and smaller until objects are no longer recognisable. Turning my attention back inside the cabin makes me present to the pungent smell of sweat, sweet odour of perfume, and the strong fumes of red wine as I examine the smooth contours of the overhead baggage compartments.

The beautiful coastline of Australia is now visible for kilometres, as it appears and disappears below the passing canvas of fluffy white cloud formations. Ascending further, now below is cloudscape and above is clear blue sky. And my mind makes its grand entry with the words and tune to the popular song 'I Can See Clearly Now'

Smiling in observation of the playful mind, I take a deep breath in, counting to four, pause, and a deep breath out, counting to six, and simply rest in pure consciousness whilst enjoying the gap until the next thought arises.

And now, I decide to have some fun with the wonders of youthfulness by using a skateboard once more – this time as the mode of transport to buy milk, bread and vegetables from the local neighbourhood grocery store. The first few pushes with one foot to build momentum of four rolling wheels on a wooden plank are a little shaky and turbulent. In this present moment, there is no room for past or future thinking. Just focusing on balancing with the left foot whilst striking the footpath with the right proves challenging enough. That motor neuron brain memory of seamlessly riding a skateboard suddenly surfaces from the archives of my 'necktop' PC and YES, I am overcome by a sense of nostalgia of being free and flying without a care in the world, now cruising towards the shops down the pathways. The mesmerising rhythm of the wheels crossing each line break in the concrete path takes me into a new dimension.

Swaying from left to right, I create an S-shape whilst whistling to the tune of 'Good Morning Starshine' by

Andy Williams and the Osmond Brothers. It is also satisfying to feel that I have done the environment a tiny favour by choosing not to drive the car this time. The hissing sound of the rubber wheels cruising down the path makes me remember those carefree childhood days when skateboards were commonly used as a mode of transport. I am now awakened to the same carefree feeling as I realise that, regardless of challenging circumstance, a deep joy always exists alongside unconditional love.

And now, in a deep meditative state during the final quadrant of the Wheel of Awareness guide meditation narrative, Deepak Chopra invites us to be present and connected to every human being and every living creature on this planet. In this current moment, considering that consciousness is non-local, I start astral travelling above the earth and among the planets in our solar system. So wonderful is the feeling to dart and float around here, there and everywhere. Words cannot describe the experience outside of time and space, however it could be likened to Being without gravity and having no identity as a male or female in formlessness.

The five senses are absent altogether; pure consciousness in the fifth dimension dominates any thoughts and I am content to just Be ... I now begin to deepen the breath and bring awareness back into the physical body. This signals a smooth descent and gradual landing back into my hands, feet, legs, arms, torso and head. Wow! What a trip that was. As I reflect on this hour-long meditation practice, I realise that once I return my physical body back to the earth, this is where I will go.

And now, mindfully walking slowly from the kitchen and preparing to travel up one flight of stairs whilst balancing a hot cup of coffee, toast and a glass of lemon water and fruit, there is little room for distracting thoughts other than taking one step at a time and keeping my gaze fixed on what is being carried in my hands.

With each step forward, a slight swaying motion occurs, forcing the liquid to wash up against the sides of the cups. Hand-eye coordination is paramount here and now as I quickly discover that with every footstep taken, a hydraulic motion within my arms is required to counterbalance the opposite movement. The left foot is elevated up onto the first step and there are twelve more to negotiate. As I glance down at the right foot to make sure it does not misjudge the second step, the breakfast begins to wobble and it almost becomes a juggling act.

Now, with only three steps to go until I am outside the bedroom door at the top of staircase, my mind decides to intervene with a question: *Wasn't that meeting in town supposed to start in thirty minutes?* At this point I become distracted, almost losing my footing, and by the grace of God, save the contents on the tray, avoiding an accident and enjoying the sumptuous breakfast in peace and quiet.

And now, being a passenger on the back of a Harley Davidson motorbike dissolves unnecessary thoughts and brings me into the present moment rather quickly. When the machine accelerates, the G-force attempts to push my body backwards as the deep growl of the engine vibrates in my heart, stomach and throat.

Holding onto the driver seems to be secondary to soaking up the surroundings as they rush past in a blur. Somehow I know that even riding around corners at a high speed on a tight angle will not throw me off the bike. The lesson here for me is not to resist a new and unusual situation and rather go with the flow. Inside the helmet I can clearly hear each breath just like an oceanic sound. This puts me into a meditative state as I become alert to each inhale and exhale.

To be in a position where the human form is moving at over eighty miles an hour, without walls or a roof for protection, is to simply trust the universe and disallow the seductive 'fear-based' thinking mind to enter the experience. A deep sense of serenity travels through me as I surrender to what is in this very moment.

And now, sitting with a seatbelt securing me next to the pilot in a helicopter, the breath deepens and is audible through the airplane headset hugging my ears. As the rotor blades gain momentum, spinning faster and faster before take-off, a rising sense of

Presence ripples through my legs and up into my torso, shoulders and head.

Gradually we lift off and sever contact with mother earth. Rising vertically, the butterflies in my stomach fly around, creating a strange, ticklish sensation. A heightened sense of awareness and alertness causes my eyelids to widen and neck to extend and rotate like a periscope. As I marvel at the scenery above, below, to the left and right of me, it strikes me yet again that consciousness is everywhere!

We move in a number of directions and hover at varying heights before travelling in a straight line above one Fiji's jungle canvases towards the largest orchid farms in the southern hemisphere. Eventually the chopper drops out of the sky and is swallowed up by the dense vegetation. "Wow," is the only word I utter to myself now as I disembark the tiny machine and make my way past a multitude of colourful orchid flowers towards the evening's final destination. On the way to the dinner tables, a beautiful choir sings native songs as I gaze up at extremely large plants on the sides of the path.

And now, disappearing from above the ground down an escalator into the Paris subway metro train system broadens my awareness to a whole new world below the earth's surface. Moments ago I could see the Eiffel Tower in the distance, and currently I am stepping off the platform and into a fast train, dimly lit, to transport me over there, somewhere.

It always fascinated me that wherever I go, be it 40,000 feet above earth or 200 feet below the earth's crust, the mind follows and consciousness remains the same. The gentle rattle of the train cabin makes me sleepy and my eyelids become heavy. Suddenly a man gets up and starts playing an accordion with gusto. It is the Edith Piaf song, 'Non, Je Ne Regrette Rien', meaning: I don't regret anything. Alertness passes through me and I flash back to being a nine-year-old boy riding home from soccer training on a similar train here in Paris.

We arrive at the Eiffel Tower stop now, and I mindfully step out of the cabin onto the station walkway. As I turn to watch the train speed away, I notice two people still inside, cursing that they failed to get off here too. They were the same distracted couple that sat quarrelling next to me and not paying attention to the Metro stops.

As I surface from the underground, I look up to see the Eiffel Tower right in front of me. The sweet smell of chestnuts wafts past my nose and crisp Parisienne air cools my scalp. There are vibrations of uneasiness passing through me, and as I keep walking closer to the landmark structure, I spot two policemen holding to the ground a man who had just attempted to steal the purse of an innocent woman. Unconsciousness and consciousness meet each other as everyone else carries on about their day.

And now, contemplating travelling over to the other side of the lake in this two-person paddleboat could be fun, yet challenging at the same time. The mind instantly throws up the obstacle of having to turn around and paddle back again.

"Seize the day!" I say, and my feet start pushing the pedals in a circular cycling motion. The water is choppy and the wind persistent, making it difficult at first to gain momentum. Before eventually settling into the present moment of what Is, I continue to wrestle with my mind as it relentlessly queries my motives.

"Are you crazy? Nobody does this!" it protests. "What happens if you are too exhausted and get stuck in the middle of the lake? You won't make it back in time to return the paddleboat and you will be fined $50!"

I proceed to paddle out into the middle of the lake. The misty drops of water from a nearby giant fountain cool my hot face and bare legs. The rocking motion of the paddle boat lengthens the gaps in between the thoughts that come and go, and although it appears I am not moving forward at all, I know that the shoreline in front of me is getting closer and closer.

And now, in this present moment I decide to travel back in time to my fourth birthday party. With eyes gently closed and sitting on a park bench, I visual the house in the Philippines, the long table that was decorated by helium balloons attached to the guests' lolly bags and my young friends arriving at the party dressed in costume. Yes, it was a fancy dress party. I was Robin and my best friend was Batman.

We ran and ran around the backyard in circles as I led the pack as the birthday boy. Energy was perpetual and laughter continual it seemed. Carefree and uninhibited, I remember vaguely only once in a while my mother and the nanny correcting me before an accident occurred.

I cannot remember any smells or tastes, however there was noise and bright colour everywhere. My sense of touch was amplified by the tropical humidity and heat of the fancy dress costume sticking to my skin. Love and joy was abundant throughout the whole birthday party and I cannot remember saying goodbye to guests as they left the house.

Nostalgia is a wonderful thing. Now, as I open my eyes and feel grateful for past experiences, I thank God. The fountain of youth floods my Being, and I get up and go about the day feeling revitalised and reenergised.

Mindlessness

In days gone by I remember not looking forward to going on trips for fear of boredom, crashing, outrageously priced tickets and delays on the journey. And when travelling, I used to mainly focus on negative things like discomfort, unsavoury food, bad service and inclement weather to name just a few. And without thinking 'outside the box', I believed that travel was restricted to a car, bicycle, plane, train or bus and was purely a necessity to get from point A to point B. Then there were frequent judgement calls I would make on other people travelling, like showing disgust at those who travelled in a more comfortable and spacious cabin class or in a more expensive car. I would also question folks who commuted on buses and trains, not realising that they were probably saving money.

Techniques to Apply

The next time you travel anywhere, be sure to take a few moments to capture the essence of the experience. Avoid being on autopilot and feeding any fears associated with your travels. Practice the ten-minute 'Body Scan Technique': with eyes opened or closed, slowly scan your body starting at your head and working your way down through each part. Be aware of what is happening in each moment.

CHAPTER 12

VACATIONING

How Mindfulness Helps

When you have spent your hard earned money on a vacation, it is worth understanding that just because you are travelling to another location like a beach, mountains in the same country or across the other side of the world, to stay in a hotel, tent, resort or on a cruise ship, that it will not necessarily solve any challenges, stress or worries you may be carrying inside you.

Being present and mindful to every experience while on holiday, starting immediately when you arrive at your destination, will not only warp time and give you an appreciation of your surroundings, but will enable you to settle into a deeper state of calmness and dissolve stress much quicker. Many people report that it takes several days just to wind down before enjoying the remainder of the holiday.

A mindfulness practice will assist to quieten the chattering mind that the daily routine back home has caused. On holiday, be attentive to the smells, sounds, sights, tastes. Be open to the cultural experiences on offer. And understand that being distracted and worrying about any issues back home is unecessary, because you will only be harming yourself and others around you.

Although I wasn't fully on holiday during the following Diary section, having joined a cruise ship to offer meditation and mindfulness sessions to passengers and crew, my family and I enjoyed the many benefits of a lifestyle away from land and routine.

The Diary

Now as the ship rocks gently left to right like a cradle during a lullaby, I become mesmerised for several minutes by the glistening sheets of water that spill over the infinity edge of the aqua-tiled pool elevated above the larger pool. It seems like liquid glass, however when I get out of the banana chair, approach the synchronized water display and place my hand into it, the crisp, cool temperature brings me to a whole new moment and feeling of Presence. The gentle murmur of the intermittent waterfall entering the pool lures me in for a refreshing dip. The taste and smell of the chlorine conflicts with the sea's salty breeze.

I return dripping wet to the comfortable chair and continue to delight in the falling glass sheets of water as the gentle tropical air dries the water drops tickling my legs and arms descending with gravity's pull. Prepared to remain in this deeply calm state of consciousness, I see my wife, Kristin, come into view out of the corner of my right eye and approach me to deliver exciting news of an art auction just commencing downstairs. As my attention shifts to giving her my full attention, the mind asks me, *What happened to that beautiful mesmerising water cascading into the pool?* I ignore the absorber of my awareness, which now would be a distraction to the present moment of listening and acknowledge what is currently very important to 'she who must be consulted'.

And now, this morning having breakfast on the back deck of Level 12, the seemingly endless panoramic ocean invokes a feeling of inner peace and deep calm as the Pacific Pearl moves through the dark blue water at 18 knots, bound for Norfolk Island. My eyes rest on a flock of five large seagulls. As they hover and glide effortlessly in a contracting formation above, curious about the activity on board, I start thinking about fellow cruiser friends, Jenny and Slade, whom I have not seen yet today. Within a few seconds they appear and both walk past me, smiling. My ear-to-ear grin takes over my face as I delight in recognition of that higher state of consciousness in play.

Following this moment, an image of my deceased father-in-law fades into my mind. So I decide to stand up and peer over the edge of the deck railing down at the sun-tanning platform below. Uncanny to note that there is an elderly man sound asleep in a chair with features almost identical to that great man who taught me many valuable life lessons and imparted so much wisdom. My body instantaneously fills with mixed feelings and sensations. My breath deepens as a montage of memories that we shared floods my mind from decades gone by. I am soon consoled by the fact we are spiritual beings having a human experience and not vice versa.

And now, by the swimming pool again, I tune in to the meditative rhythm of the song 'Black Betty' and observe several passengers clap their hands together to the catchy musical notes. I witness with delight collective consciousness dancing amongst life, free from worries. These upbeat vibes are contagious. In a playful way, my body starts jiving to the music as I eventually overcome the ego and rise up to join the youthful group in dance. Uninhibited in this present moment, my arms, neck and head are thrashing around to the frantic rhythm as I become camouflaged amongst the skimpily-clothed human beings.

As I shake out all inhibitions from my mind and physical body, there is an overwhelming sense of tranquillity and peace within. The music appears to be muffled and everyone's movements seem to be in slow motion. Maybe I have entered a higher state of consciousness independent of thought? Whatever it is, I am thoroughly enjoying being in the moment. Looking up at the light blue sky adds a new dimension, giving me an out-of-body experience outside of time and space.

I highly recommend being a dancing body on a floating vessel in the middle of an ocean among happy people to realise even for a fleeting moment a unity consciousness, where everything fuses into one experience.

And now, during the samba dance class in the Dome at the front of the majestic floating community, I observe and participate in the count of 1,2,3 Pause, 7,8,9 soft landing beats of small foot movements with subtle hip swings. 'The Girl From Ipanema' tune appears in my mind and creates conflict with the existing music playing on the ship's stereo system. To focus on any other than the present footstep, would force a mini collision with the dancing passengers next to me. The limbic resonance between dance teacher and passengers begins to harmonise like a conductor and the orchestra. I decide to leave the dance class and meditate instead.

Now in a visualization meditative state seated at the front of the Pacific Pearl's top deck, my eyes squint to filter the almost blinding, glistening ocean shimmer from the mid-afternoon sun reflection, as it seems to ripple in slow motion. For several minutes I enjoy no more than the bliss and unity of synchronizing my breath's inhales and exhales with the rising and falling of Her Majesty as she travels confidently through the thick, syrup-like consistency of deep water. The gap in between thoughts is getting longer and longer, and the beauty of absolute nothingness is everything as I rest in Being.

Now I wake to the Captain's announcement that the waters are too choppy and dangerous to dock and disembark passengers at Norfolk Island, so we are circumnavigating the formal penal colony before making our way back to Sydney. In the past I would have reacted with frustration and disappointment, however now I feel totally at peace with the Captain's decision and full of gratitude that we are able to at least view the lush green hilly landscape of the island.

Overlooking the balcony of the top deck now, I feel proud for acknowledging and processing this morning's news in a way that probably completely bypassed my brain's amygdala. I overhear other passengers in a state of anxiety and bitter disappointment about not being able to set foot on land for at least another day. With compassion, I introduce the STOP method to a couple standing next to me:

- Stop
- Take three breaths in and out and smile
- Observe your body
- Proceed with care to yourself and others

They look at me with mysterious eyes as I walk towards the seemingly endless buffet breakfast.

In a state of panic, other passengers express concern that they will be unable to purchase souvenirs from this historical island. In my calm amongst the external chaos of this 'first world problem', I give thanks to God for a pair of eyes that can see the pristine landscape clearly from afar.

And now, finding Jacob, the ship's art director, is proving a challenge. Inspired by my long-time favourite artist, Salvador Dali, I wonder if it may be worth investing in a unique painting or sketch of his. I browse through the gallery, contemplating the difference in price between an 'original' and a 'unique' piece of artwork. At the risk of overthinking, I imagine and visualise the feelings on approach to the chosen framed piece that may eventually decorate my living room wall. As I discretely usher myself onto a seat during a presentation on the artwork of famous American artist, Thomas Kinkade, I spot Jacob out of the corner of my left eye, signalling with thumbs up that he likes the Dali T-shirt I'm sporting. Knowing that radical creativity and intuition are elements of higher states of consciousness, I feel excited about the conversation soon to unfold.

As inspiring and enlightening is the work of Kinkade in the present moment, my mind is persistently trying to lure me into the future discussion I will soon have concerning my interest in the price and accessibility of a unique Dali sketch or painting. The tug-of-war between present moment and the future ensues for another thirty minutes until the presentation concludes.

Now perusing the wonderful Painter of Light Kinkade's paintings, I catch Jacob's eye and we discuss which unique Dali pieces are available within my budget. Thankfully, right now nothing is available, which is just as well, because I don't have the money anyway.

And now, Kristin and I make our way down to sit on the back deck of Level 10. Watching the gentle movements of the varnished wooden handrail meet the eye line of the Pacific Ocean horizon transcends me into a deeper state of calm. Then doing a headstand for fun and seeing the world upside down puts a different perspective on life in these very moments with deep blue ocean up there and the light blue sky down below. Consciousness remains the same as I feel gravity move blood down my legs towards my head in a rejuvenating fashion.

Moments later and back in the deck chair, I think to myself it would be nice to go for a swim. Seconds later, Kristin suggests we go for a swim. Amusing … Floating in the refreshing crystal clear water now, I start wondering why I have not seen my teenage daughter since she woke up this morning, and within seconds she is waltzing past us with her friend, waving. Wonderful … I start chuckling in wonderment at a pattern emerging of events occurring just after I have thought about them.

I believe the good news is that eventually one is able to maintain a deeper state of calm, joy and focus, not only on a relaxing cruise holiday, but in everyday life, by applying a continual mindfulness practice to daily living and simple tasks.

And now, it dawns on me that the meditation and mindfulness sessions I am conducting on this cruise for passengers and the executive crew respectively completes the holistic nature of care and attention on offer to enhance our lifestyles. From entertainment to healthy, tasty food, acupuncture, massage, teeth whitening, gait analysis and inner sole shoe inserts, metabolism and liver cleansing solutions, hairstyling, mind games, artwork, historical and geographic educational lectures, fitness regimes and matchmaking, I am grateful to be of service addressing the care of 'being' above the canvas of busy minds, by helping people to access their consciousness and sense of Presence that is ever so patient, still and knowing.

During this particular teaching session, I explain to cruisers that unless we peel back all the layers of each of our onions and address any underlying issues causing pain to our bodies, egos and old belief systems at the core of Being, no amount of superficial solutions will give us the ultimate bliss and internal joy we all deserve.

Several passengers thank me for guiding them down the path towards deeper happiness, enhanced focus, and a calmer sense of being. They become enlightened to know that freedom is not only being on vacation at sea on a ship, but that they are also free for every present moment of their lives.

And now, I reflect on a comment made by the on-board fitness instructor:

"Make the most of it here on the cruise while you are free, because soon you won't be after you get off the ship."

In fact, I beg to differ. Freedom exists in each and every one of us twenty-four hours a day, seven days a week, if we live in the present moment and cease identifying with the mind and its past and future worries that can torment and stress us out. Back in the cabin, in complete silence I sit cross-legged on the bed, staring at the ripples in the crisp bed sheets, waiting patiently for the next pearl of wisdom to arise...

Aha, yes, the fitness instructor is still young and gaining life experience, hence the flippant comment about the lack of freedom existing in the external world. So I decide to leave him a note at the front desk to call me and have a discussion around the topic of freedom that exists within each human being's inner space, regardless of circumstances externally.

I gaze softly at the knit design in the blanket in a restful position for a while and become enlightened to the fact that I cannot change the world, but I can care for people and their wellbeing by being the messenger, pointer and guide towards a better life.

And now, it is almost time to disembark the ship and return home after eighteen days at sea. As I try to close the zipper around my suitcase, it becomes apparent that the accumulation of souvenirs during this island-hopping vacation is causing an overspill of contents. So I realise that I need to be even more mindful when repacking the suitcase now so everything will fit neatly and it can be sealed. By observing the shapes, sizes and textures of clothing, shoes, adventure gear and various artefacts, a more effective method of packing can be applied. It reminds me of a jigsaw puzzle or the game, Tetris, where the next piece laid down must fit into the contours of both the space and the previous item.

Yes, it is a test of patience and there is considerable thought involved with the exercise. Being innovative, I stuff socks, T-shirts and small souvenir items inside the shoe cavities to maximise space. Once laid in the suitcase flush against the sides, other softer items are moulded around the shoes. Long pants and larger clothing is laid flat and layered along the entire length of the case. The snorkel can be slotted into the corner, and finally mask and diving flippers are pressed hard against everything else.

Ahh, then I turn around to see a sports jacket hiding behind me. Taking a deep breath in and out, I carefully fold it in half, place it on top of the flippers, tuck the edges in and start lifting the suitcase up and shaking it from side to side, allowing gravity to help me settle the contents into every nook and cranny. And zip, zip, zip. This time the suitcase closes effortlessly.

Mindlessness

Before my transformation occurred to Present Moment Living, a holiday like this was consumed with constant distractions, which entailed missing many precious moments. In fact, sometimes I went on holidays and only vaguely remembered what happened.

"Gee," I would say, "That was way too short a time. There wasn't really much to see or do and I still feel stressed out!" Even on holiday I was consumed with always looking at emails and worrying about work situations and the To Do lists I'd need to tackle on my return. I cheated myself financially and spiritually of a perfectly good 'get away' from the day-to-day routines of life.

Techniques to apply

And now, recall a wonderful time you had on vacation and journal the nostalgia and details of activity that occurred in those present moments. Next time you take a vacation, just be grateful and observant to where you are, what you are doing, and how you are feeling, and adopt a youthful outlook to all experiences as they unfold every minute of the day and night.

CHAPTER 13

KNOWING & BEING

How Mindfulness Helps

A fter adopting a regular mindfulness practice, you may find that your intuition becomes more finely tuned and your sense of 'knowing' increases. And it is by 'being' more and 'doing' less that Present Moment Living becomes effortless and second nature. Frequently you get a hunch that something is about to happen. For example, you know that there will be a parking space waiting for you in a crowded car park, or you think of your best friend whom you haven't spoken to in months and the phone rings and it is her. You also become very comfortable simply sitting still in silence and Being. It feels better than being on holiday, lying down on a banana chair on a tropical white sandy beach, sipping a cocktail in the sunshine.

The Diary

And now, I am supposed to make a seemingly important phone call overseas. On my way upstairs to fetch the mobile phone before preparing the evening meal, I hear a shout downstairs that indicates the dishwasher just stopped working. Processing that news leaves me in a state of bemusement. I reach for my iPhone and press the On button, only to find the battery is completely drained of power despite it being 90% charged only thirty minutes ago.

Hmm, interesting, I think as I ponder this peculiarity. So now, I go to turn on the fully charged iPad to find the phone number that I need to make the call. Its battery is also out of charge. Beyond coincidence, I see these occurrences as a sign that I need to fix the dishwasher, cook the evening meal and be present for my children. Once upon a time, I would have escalated the situation, with my pain body kicking into 'fight mode' and exploding with a temper tantrum in frustration. Cortisol would have flooded my brain with its nasty effects on my physical body. And then again, this is just a story in my mind.

So now I laugh to myself and delight in gratitude for awareness to the broader universe in play. It is uncanny that a yoga student of mine just rang the doorbell unannounced. She declares that her husband's intense anxiety attacks are getting out of control and wonders if I can quickly suggest some techniques that can assist him to return to a calm state of being. I make some recommendations.

On reflection of this recent sequence of events, I acknowledge and am grateful for God's intervention and the intelligence of the rearranging forces of the universe to put me in a position of ultimate service to others. I later make the overseas phone call and apologise for the delay.

And now, sitting on the earth at the summit of a hill with a 360-degree view of Canberra, I know that within minutes there will be darkness as the sun sets for another day. Being alert and attentive to ever-changing shadow shapes cast off rocks and trees gives rise to Presence. The clouds and colours in the sky shift subtly, moment by moment.

A thought or two steals my attention elsewhere. When I look back at the sky, the clouds are in a very different formation. Knowing that shortly I won't be able to see the surrounding nature beyond my feet, I pay extra attention to the movement of wildlife overlayed by the symphony of birds heralding the end of another day's light.

Dusk appears and begins welcoming the magic hour when shadows can no longer be seen. The smell of pinecones and tree sap reveals itself. The temperature drops as the light of the sun fades and a soothing air chill massages my skin lightly. Consciousness becomes ever noticeable and seems more prominent as sights and sounds diminish into the new night and detachment from the human form becomes apparent. Well, there goes yet another blip on the universe's continuum.

And now, for the second time I open the refrigerator door to look for the packet of chia seeds that I am using as a key ingredient in a fruit smoothie. Knowing the packet is somewhere in there hidden among everything else, I close the door and reach for a banana on the bench easily visible and convenient to skin, break in pieces and drop into the electric blender. During this phase of producing my 'temple cleansing' concoction, the mind interferes and suggests how silly I am that even after looking for the chia seeds twice in such a confined space, they were still not found. Slightly irritated, I sigh and proceed to open the fridge door again, determined to identify and capture the chia seeds within a couple of seconds. With a quick scan of the food from the top to bottom shelves and door cavities, I let the heavy stainless steel door swing shut empty handed.

Yanking open the freezer door, I see the blueberries straightaway. A handful of this precious antioxidant rich food is tossed into the mix. A pinch of brain-shaped walnuts are added, along with spoonfuls of macca and cocoa powder. But still no chia seeds in sight! So I take a deep breath in and a longer exhale, approach the fridge one last time, mindfully observe with fresh eyes and attention to items on the top shelf, and right in front of me, next to the cheese, is a plastic Tupperware container with chia seeds inside. Someone in the house had removed this nourishing food from the original packet. I chuckle in amusement that things never stay the same and are always subject to change.

And now, in the local department store, there is a quietness and emptiness that surrounds the clothes racks on the New Year's Day afternoon. In the changing room, Kristin is trying on a pair of jeans that I may be buying for her birthday. Sitting quietly and waiting patiently, just looking and listening, I notice a young shop assistant providing advice to a customer about a garment and how to care for it. She appears to be extra joyous about life with a very enlightened way of Being. She has a permanent smile on her face whilst gliding around the clothing section and I know it is not because she is working in the holiday season on the first day of the year. There is something touching her life. She is all lit up!

When I eventually approach the counter to pay for Kristin's birthday jeans, this shop assistant is definitely glowing with a sense of Presence. I greet her with a "Happy New Year". She grins and starts to mindfully place the folded jeans into a shopping bag. After paying for the gift, I hand it to Kristin and wish her Happy Birthday. The young sales assistant lights up immediately and shares that today is also her birthday and that she will be celebrating as soon as her afternoon shift is over. It is so delightful at this moment witnessing two people on the first day of the calendar year laughing together about their shared birthdays. I believe it is no coincidence that two New Year's babies unite.

And now, as people stream into the hall to attend the Shift in Consciousness teaching session I am leading, there is a soulful enlightened person at the back assisting me with ushering attendees to their seats after taking their entry fees. Deral just instinctively knows how to be of service. I never asked for her assistance and yet she mindfully and kindly leads with initiative and compassion in a seemingly effortless way, floating across the room, coordinating extra chairs, photography and even a coffee and slice of banana bread for me prior to the event.

There are many extraordinary things about this human being who appears very grateful for life. She is obviously highly respected within the community as many people greet her with big hugs and broad smiles.

Halfway through the teaching session during the guided meditation section, I notice Deral in the back row, slumping in a sleeping position. Her physical body obviously needs the rest. After the teaching session I talk to her and learn that she manages a family of five, the town's premiere fitness centre and a new wellness retreat venture.

Soulful people like this operate at a higher state of consciousness, achieve a lot and make everything look so effortless. When I thank Deral for her generous assistance, she responds with a warm smile and proclaims that it was no problem and a sheer pleasure to be of service.

And now, Luke appears in the foyer of the hotel to meet me for dinner in Sydney. Having known him for over thirty-five years as my best friend since we were young teenagers, makes for yet another great catch-up in the present moment. A firm grip handshake takes place, a few words are exchanged and we proceed to wander down to the Oyster Bar. What is remarkable apart from the general conversation about family, work, sport and current affairs, is we are simply Being in each other's company outside of time and space.

It is typical when we meet up either for a phone call or in person that several hours go by without even knowing it. Now, there is a bond of collective consciousness and Presence resounding through our physical form bodies as we each sip a glass of French red wine and stare across the water towards the Harbour Bridge. After several minutes of silence, we start to speak at exactly the same time. We are naturally 100% attentive to each other and mystically have never had any attachment to each other's ego in a competitive sense.

We start recalling funny and adventurous moments from our childhood and discuss some of the mischievous events we orchestrated together when we were in college. During that time, I believe Luke was much more present than me. He seems to be able to remember much more of the happenings than I can.

And now, speaking in the French language, I notice that the person I am conversing with is looking at me and responding in a way that is no different to the English I started the conversation with. Yes, practising French is straining my brain somewhat, and what is pleasant to note is the observer – consciousness is the same universally, regardless of the spoken audible word. And by being in this mode, I am not thinking ahead about what the conversion of words from my mother tongue of English will be in French.

So at present, the French words keep flowing effortlessly and almost fluently. Deep down in my mind's archive lies the memory of this romantic language I first learnt as a child whilst living in Paris over four decades ago.

The playful side of Being, surfaces and expresses itself to the other person. *"Avec chaque verre de vin rouge, mon Français est plus meilleur"* which roughly translates to, "With each glass of red wine, my French becomes much better". My love affair with life in this moment converts to a bellowing laugh and reminds me that knowing another language is handy yet superficial, because at the end of the day, it is universal consciousness that matters most.

And now, I stop jogging along the nature trail, regain my natural breath and simply rest in Being. As I spend the next few minutes surrounded by the great Australian sun-scorched bushland, I become aware of birds in trees camouflaged by the foliage and sets of shiny kangaroo eyes and fluffy ears poking up above long wild grass. The longer I remain still and quiet whilst observing nature, the more I see, smell and hear. Just over there is a brown snake's tail protruding from a hollow log. Ants are marching on a journey to somewhere.

Presence intensifies within and around my body. Gradually my legs feel like they are rooted in the earth like a tree trunk, a wider variety of sounds is amplified and smaller furry animals, an echidna and an assortment of insects become curious about me.

The dimension of Oneness with the surroundings fuses my whole experience together, and in this moment a feeling of bliss, sense of gratitude and joy overwhelm my being. I marvel in awe with a few tears at the creation of the universe and acknowledge the trillions and trillions of atoms that make up everything I know.

And now, having picked up my eldest son, Jesper, from the international airport, we sit next to each other just being in silence. It is midnight; I have not seen him physically for almost a year because he has been living on the other side of the planet in Sweden. Using audible words with vowels and syllables to catch up on what has occurred since we last saw each other isn't necessary. As we sip our drinks and nibble on crackers and cheese, several minutes pass in silence as we continue to bond as father and son in a state of unity and collective consciousness.

The harmonics and repetitive rhythm of the background music puts both of us in a transcendental state. With each beat of the sound, we sway in unison from left to right, glancing across at each other from time to time. Eventually we simultaneously burst out in laughter, then give each other a big hug, declaring that it is great to see each other again.

As Jesper tells me about his recent adventures and career developments overseas, I remain fully attentive to his every word. My mind now reminds me that for years as he was growing up I would be distracted by other thoughts whenever he wanted my attention. For a fleeting moment I observe that thought and associated past flashbacks, before being 100% present for my son.

And now, instead of growing impatient and frustrated by waiting for family members to leave the house and get in the car to drive to a destination at an agreed time, I simply rest in Being by sitting in the car alone until others join me. It is actually an opportunity in disguise to come to stillness. I close my eyes whilst resting my brain yet maintaining an alertness and awareness to the surroundings.

Several minutes pass and my mind tempts me to beep the car horn as a 'hurry up' signal to the others. A deeper breath in and out brings me back to a centred way of Being. A broader awareness steps in and I start hearing the faint sounds of voices, footsteps and a dog barking. Moment by moment the sounds grow louder and now in the rear view mirror I see two people with a Chihuahua stroll past down the footpath.

Suddenly I start noticing dirt stains on parts of the vehicle that normally are not visible to me, more than likely because I never sat still for long enough to notice them.

Finally, family members approach the car and I feel a sense of joy for their Presence and the opportunity to choose Being and not Frustration.

And now, almost one year after deciding to become the world's first person to run a half marathon in a hot-air balloon, I am taking small strides on a treadmill powered by a generator within the confined space of the basket. The pilot is behind me, steering the vessel and the engineer/photographer is standing in the other compartment next to me.

What an incredible, surreal experience it is to be running suspended over 1,000 feet above the earth's surface and at the same time raise money for the Heart Foundation. This will make an entertaining film clip on YouTube to watch one day.

As nature's forces move me peacefully from left to right, up and down at will, I observe that consciousness is the same up here among the clouds as it is down there on the earth.

A phone call comes in from a local radio station to check on my progress. Almost breathless, with mobile phone pressed against one ear, I report that the scenery is absolutely breathtaking and reminds me of the dreams I had as a child flying, and that this adventure is one of the most unique ways to raise funds for a charity organisation. The present moment appears endless.

Mindlessness

Once upon a time, I would have said that the notion of knowing what will happen was reserved for clairvoyants and witches. My sheer ignorance and lack of education about mindfulness and meditation practices led me to believe I knew everything there was to know about life. 'Being' to me used to be a waste of time, laziness, and represented a person looking like a zombie rocking gently backward and forward in a catatonic state. The old belief system taught me that there was no time to waste and people in society should always be doing, doing, doing if they weren't sleeping.

Techniques to Apply

Practice sitting still and being silent first for one minute, then five minutes, then ten minutes and keep increasing the time as the days go by. This could be done alone or in a group. Observe half a walnut in silence and journal your findings. Reflect on the difference between what your mind is telling you and what your heart is saying. Become aware of sensations in your body at the moment you are about to make a decision. Trust your 'gut instinct'.

CHAPTER 14

CONNECTING

How Mindfulness Helps

A mindfulness practice and living in the present moment offers access to a more subtle world – not seen by the human eye – as well as a new kind of connection with people and living creatures. The best part of consistently living in the present moment on purpose and non-judgementally is that you connect with different levels of consciousness and gradually find yourself living in multidimensional consciousness. The law of attraction begins to favour you on a daily basis and life becomes more colourful, whilst more opportunities present themselves via connections with people and circumstances.

The Diary

And now, I am present to the moments during the Wheel of Awareness guided meditation pointer in the fourth quadrant: *Relations and connections with people in my life*. I visualise having a neighbourhood party. Having reflected on this several times over the last couple of months, one day there is a knock at the door from next-door neighbour, Monica. When I open the door, I sense she is going to ask me something about a gathering of some sort. A flashback from a previous meditation session I experienced surfaces: *Be aware of your connection and relationships in your neighbourhood.*

"I think it would be a good idea if we finally have a neighbourhood party after all these years, don't you?" says Monica, smiling.

So recognising yet again, another example of flowing with the current of heightened consciousness and synchronicity, I smile back and agree to hosting a gathering for our collective home dwellings on either sides of our houses and across the other side of the road. It was Deepak Chopra who taught me how to expand the 'hub of awareness' by practicing the Wheel of Awareness guided meditation (authored originally by Dr Daniel Siegel).

And I can see why it has given rise to unity and collective consciousness now in my neighbourhood. Also, having recently returned from a five-day retreat conducted by Eckhart Tolle, I am acutely aware of the Presence that exists moment by moment, as Consciousness unites in the near distance, manifested by more than twenty-five human beings of all ages and nationalities walking towards my house for a congregation of togetherness, whilst entertained with food, drinks, music, fun and laughter.

What fascinates me is that although some of us are geographically located close enough to be heard with a slight raised voice, we are awakened to the fact that we haven't actually conversed in years. In fact, a few guests don't even realise the new friends with whom they are socialising live in the house diagonally opposite. It dawns on me that in today's society, we get so caught up in the 'doing' and 'unnecessary thinking', becoming fragmented, that we lose sight of the overarching collective consciousness, whilst unconsciously ignoring our closest surrounding neighbours.

So now, the Ginnivan/Brown neighbourhood party is in full swing. As we huddle cosily under the front porch with a variety of drinks and finger food in hand, we talk to each other harmoniously, sharing experiences, identifying common interests and generally enjoying ourselves.

I take a few moments to step into the light shower of rain and feel a strong sense of Presence arising as drops of water land on my bald head, as I observe a new network of energy being woven among the neighbourhood. The collective murmur of sound exiting their mouths appears willing and unforced in a way that suggests we have all been suppressing this collective connection right here and now for too many years.

As I step back into the group, Ben from the house across the road on the left side offers me a glass of red wine. I accept gladly and also comment on his crystal wine goblet, guessing it was won in a golf tournament.

"How did you know?" he replies in astonishment.

I then think to myself that this could be yet another example of synchronicity and intuition in play.

And now, outside on the back deck, I sit after a sumptuous dinner observing a star jasmine plant that over time has crawled up a wall on the side of the house. I know there is oneness and unity of consciousness within us because when the cool evening breeze caresses the vines, they respond with gentle movements, which in turn ripple wonderful waves of energy into my body. I feel a sense of joy as the little white five-petal flowers seem to smile at me and amplify their Presence like something out of *Alice's Adventures In Wonderland*.

Silence and stillness pervade for a few seconds and then here comes another breeze, moving across the dark green crawler and causing a Mexican wave among the flowers. I grin from ear to ear in awe of nature and its harmony as well as the cheekiness of my mind suggesting that observers may surmise I was on a hallucinogenic drug of some kind.

Stillness appears again and this time a rising sense of Presence and anticipation arises within my physical body just before the next wave of gentle breeze caresses the star jasmine vines again. It is priceless to acknowledge and understand how consciousness indeed exists within plant life at large.

And now, on a bushwalk, a stop to observe an anthill of significant size. By watching the army of thousands of busy insects methodically making its way in and out of holes in the dirt mound, I feel the rising of Presence within and a fused sense of unity consciousness existing in this moment. Mesmerised by the waves of mass movement, I decide to focus my vision on just one particular red ant, who makes his way over and around his fellow creatures. *I wonder what mission he is on?* I speculate, wishing I knew his purpose.

By continuing to be in the moment with every move of his powerful legs, I am drawn closer to the insect city, and decide to place my hand fearlessly onto the mound. Instantly several ants, including the one I had been following, climb all over my fingers. A ticklish sensation travels up my forearm towards my shoulder, as they march to investigate this intrusion. With my Fight or Flight response kicking in, I now observe the ants making their way back down my arm and back to home base.

I wonder why my skin wasn't bitten. Maybe the smelly odour from my armpit deterred them from proceeding any further up my body? I brush off the remaining ants from my unscathed arm and proceed to continue my walk down the dirt fire trail.

And now, the bossa nova song – 'The Girl from Ipanema' travels through the loud speakers and enters my ears, vibrating like a gentle sea breeze throughout my head. Looking out of the dining room window, past the outdoor table and grassy green lawn, white fairy lights dance in a swaying fashion hanging from the bush wall against the back fence. To feel connection between sound harmonics, light and nature, places me in an alert yet mesmerised state of cosmic consciousness. As the wind comes and goes, it seems that the movement caused amongst the lights and plants are aligned to the rhythms of the seductive Brazilian tune.

A deeper feeling of peace and harmony delivers me to the familiar place of joy and Being. It actually feels like I am receiving a gentle brain massage. In fact, I am present to pleasant sensations as if every organ and cell in my physical body is being caressed with love and care.

And just like that, my mind whisks me away to a powdery white sandy beach overlooking crystal clear aqua waters shimmering against the warm sunlight. A whiff of coconut oil passes my nose as a tanned girl in a bikini strolls past, swaying her hips from side to side. A deep breath in and out brings me back to silence and pure consciousness for several more moments.

And now, there is an opportunity to acquaint myself with all the details that decorate and make up the character of the house's living room, while waiting for Annika to finish her homework before taking the dog for a walk. Sitting on the leather sofa and observing the ornaments, framed photos and paintings decorating the walls and mantelpiece, eventually brings my attention to the tall indoor palm tree potted in a terracotta pot featuring an Aztec design. It suddenly becomes apparent that I am observing so much more detail in a room that I have walked through time and time again but never stopped to pay attention to the surroundings.

Looking at the tree's ringed trunk first, then allowing my eyes to wander up towards the thin leaves, initiates a flash of nostalgia. The memory of having purchased this plant twenty years ago surfaces, and it dawns on me that it has been part of the furniture for all this time, having always lived in the living room.

I reach over and place my hand around its trunk and rest in stillness. Good and bad memories flood into my mind where situations and events occurred in its Presence. I feel God consciousness in this moment. I then come to the realization that, over the years, everyone in the house has bothered to water it except me. With a newfound connection to one of the family's longest living associates, I fetch a jug of water and pour it into the pot and watch the soil drink it all up.

And now, I gaze at the near half moon getting brighter moment by moment in the clear sky, as the sun continues to set behind the horizon. For fun, I attempt the yoga pose – half moon – by planting my straight left leg and left arm on the ground whilst lifting my right leg and right arm in the air. The sky's colours morph from blue to faded mauve as the sun sinks down further. Momentarily I spy some kind of face created by the shadows on this wondrous planet.

There is no wind and my mind mirrors the stillness and serenity of the evening.

Squinting while staring at the moon creates a halo effect in the shape of a cross surrounding it. I feel like reaching up to hold the moon and bring it closer to earth. As I lift my hand higher and pretend to grab the moon, an electrical field of universal energy travels down my arm.

Just looking into the sky for several more moments, I spot the first star shining against increasing darkness. Then another appears, and another, and another. The balance of the universe occurs subtly with dark, dissolving light.

The volume of Presence is amplified now, as the calm night is speckled with countless stars. When I stop counting the stars, I feel totally at one with the universe. In fact, I know I am part of the universe.

And now, while removing cobwebs from the outdoor window frames of the house, I am confronted by a venomous redback spider that the feather duster has swept to the ground. My reptilian brain's first reaction is to either flee or squash the dangerous insect. Instead

I mindfully observe its movements and understand that this eight-legged creature is part of Australia's natural habitat and means no harm unless it finds itself under threat or is looking for food.

It starts crawling towards me and I decide to calmly place my hand on the ground in front of its path to see what happens. The spider proceeds to crawl up my hand. My breath deepens, heated bodily sensations arise and my heartbeat increases as my mind screams, *What in the hell are you doing? Don't you know you could get very sick and even die if you are bitten?* The black creature pauses for a moment and then continues crawling across the back of my hand before making contact with the earth again and walking away.

Needless to say, this is one of my most memorable present moment experiences to be cherished as a oneness experience with nature. Please don't try this at home, kids!

And now, sitting in the car, waiting for a couple of running buddies to join me for a drive to the cross country racing track, two dragonflies fly into sight, hovering outside the front window. With fascination, I observe that they are both connected to each other while manoeuvring gracefully left to right, forward and backward. There is an obvious curiosity on their part as to something within the vehicle, because they repeatedly fly into the windshield.

Amazingly these bizarre insects are not becoming disconnected when crashing into the window. There is some kind of commitment to stay together: perhaps they are mating? My eyes follow their travels as they move quickly into the distance, taken by a sudden gust of wind before coming to land on a wispy flower stem to investigate it for a moment. Then off they go again, still attached to each other, and fly far into the distance until I can no longer see them.

Now reflecting on the connection between the two dragonflies, I become enlightened yet again to an experience where no outside unnecessary pervasive thoughts took place during these moments of paying utmost attention to their curious dance. A heightened sense of awareness is ever present right now.

And now, as I sit quietly writing on a bench at the beach with the sound of waves and smell of sea salt opening up my creativity and alertness, a young woman appears in front of me and starts hanging wet clothing out to dry on the wooden handrail behind the sand bank. After a few minutes, she sits down next to me and starts explaining in a heavy German accent that she and her friend over there in that van are in transit as backpackers, venturing around the north and south-eastern coasts of Australia.

Intrigued, I ask whether they knew each other in Germany before coming to the land down under. Katarina replies that they only met by chance and formed a real connection that cannot be described in words. In a robust conversation, we discuss favourite beaches on the south coast and are delighted to collectively agree that Surf Beach here and now is the best by far.

Katarina says that it is nice to simply spend time relaxing in the sun, in no hurry to get somewhere whilst waiting for her clothes to dry. With nowhere to be other than right here, we choose to sit in silence and reflect on each and every moment. A slight breeze creates mild movement and a whispering sound among the drying clothes that hang loose. There is certainly not a moment being missed.

And now, on an orange plantation in a rural country town, I am invited to pick my very first fruit from one of the trees. The sense of anticipation and Presence heightens within, as I have never done this before. I walk towards a tree full of lush, bright-coloured oranges, feeling exhilarated. Within arm's reach now, I gently grab the round fruit from the base and after careful instruction, mindfully twist it anticlockwise before it effortlessly separates itself from its life force branch. The vibrant energy of the orange resting in my hand is very different to the lifelessness I have experienced holding a supermarket orange.

With both hands I wrap my arms around the fruit tree and feel a connection of unity consciousness like we are fused together in one experience. In gratitude I thank the tree silently for gracefully parting with a piece of its juicy Vitamin C goodness that provides sustenance in so many ways.

On close inspection the outer skin of the orange has a few dark blotches and dents. As I break it open, a burst of sweet citrus ignites and liquid drops land on my face. The slithers of fleshy, tangy orange are so incredibly tasty. They also quench my thirst on such a scorching hot summer's day.

In this present moment, I am realising that beauty is deeper than the skin that surrounds life itself. Although the orange skin is blemished, the inside content is nourishing and life-giving.

Mindlessness

Living a fragmented life in isolation from others and not caring about anyone except myself was my old way of being. Every time I heard someone say they made a connection with someone new or an animal or plant, my mind proclaimed in judgement, *Another bloody flower power hippy!* I thought that the world and humanity would take care of itself without any other connection taking place. "What you see is what you get" were words uttered out of my mouth frequently. And many times I wasn't even aware or believed that a connection existed outside of anything tangible or visible to the human eye.

Techniques to Apply

Notice three situations each day where people make connections with others or their pets and simply observe. Take a few minutes during a lunch break to notice a bird or an insect connecting with another, or consider nature in general and the impact it has on the world. Make some notes in your journal about your observations.

CHAPTER 15

WONDERING

How Mindfulness Helps

A mindfulness practice helps you to become more naturally curious and wonder about the unknown or undiscovered. For it is only the mind that can stop you from wondering. As being mindful assists in being non-judgmental and open minded, we then develop tendencies to inquire about something until we find the answers. That wonderment of a child surfaces and we feel comfortable exploring what might be.

Because in the present moment everything appears more detailed and interesting, wondering becomes a form of entertainment and education. Eventually a discovery is made, and sometimes leads to breakthroughs in life, and solutions for problems.

The Diary

And now, strolling in the park whilst tapping into the quietness of my inner space, I walk towards a hollow log lying on the ground and stop to observe its character. In this stillness and state of being, eventually a faint rustling sound is heard from within the log. Feeling curious, I decide to sit down alongside the old fallen tree branch. Moments pass before I hear the same scratching noise inside. It appears to be the home of a mammal, reptile or large insect. Resting my hand on top of the log, I feel an aliveness that sends good feelings down my arm and into my body, eventually surfacing in my face as a smile.

After a few more moments, the noise from within gets louder and the sound travels towards the entrance of the log. A black pointy nose is now poking out of the hole, followed by the head of an echidna. I stare at it in sheer delight as it stares back at me. We lock gazes momentarily before it scurries back into what appears to be its home. Now a flurry of activity sends vibrations and sounds up and down the log shaft. My mind queries whether the spikey, blackish-brown animal is excited or angry to see me sitting here. A deeper breath in, and acknowledgment of deeper breath out, brings the peace of pure consciousness to the foreground. I reflect on this creature's existence on earth.

And now, while I'm sitting on the back deck and simply Being, a duck waddles towards me from the distance and continues until it stops only a few feet away. It stares at me. Then two black and white magpies fly in from seemingly nowhere and perch themselves in a tree above my head. There they too look down at me. I start smiling, wondering why a sudden congregation of feathered friends has gathered around me, up close and personal. I sense this is a beautiful experience beyond coincidence. Whilst looking into their eyes and feeling unity consciousness, another two birds of a species unknown to me land next to the duck and also join in the game of wonderment.

As I chuckle to myself, feeling extremely blissful and at one with nature, the Carpenters' song 'Close To You' enters my mind.

It dawns on me that the 'you' in the song is Consciousness. Fascinating to note that my mind gains momentum by inquiring about these wonderful feathered creatures until they decide it is all too intrusive, so simultaneously they all fly away. No surprise, I gather?

And now, walking to the car being present to the surroundings, I look to the clear sky and my attention is grabbed by the most beautiful floral creation emerging from the middle of a flax plant above my eyeline. Not knowing what it is, I marvel at its unique shape and thin offshoots covered in white flower buds. My mind asks, *Is a giant flower with hundreds of mini flower buds sprouting in all directions from the dark brown stem?*

As I gently feel the delicate, rubbery-textured buds, a deep sense of unity, heightened awareness and Presence fills my body. A hovering bee now visits the unknown creation. In search of nature's sweetness, the insect floats above several slightly opened flower buds before carefully selecting its sweet produce. As I lean forward to smell the wonder of nature basking in the sunlight, the golden bee investigates my eyebrow before returning to the mysterious crown of many sweetened nutritious pockets of pollen.

As I stroke the universe's creation with my hand, it responds with a gentle rocking sway from side to side. A vibrant yet peaceful serenity fuses with the energy being generated through my fingertips, and both corners of my mouth lift up, creating a smile from ear to ear.

And now, I remember Eckhart Tolle saying to look up at the sky to feel an amplified sense of Presence. So I tilt my head up, resting it on the back of this outdoor chair and gaze at the a blue sky covered by a moving patchwork of white clouds. What quickly catches my attention is the graceful, silent shape-changing nature of the clouds.

Because its formation continually evolves and dissolves moment by moment, I become mesmerised in wonderment at the experience that I cannot label with words. This next cloud makes a shape that resembles a dog with floppy ears. I laugh to myself as I observe my playful monkey mind that disrupted the gap of consciousness for a few seconds. I switch my attention to a different cloud formation that does not resemble anything familiar to me, and another beautiful, serene gap of peaceful 'nothingness' appears in between thoughts.

A moment of clarity surfaces out of consciousness to answer a question I have harboured for many years. I continue to sit in stillness for a while longer, just in case more moments of clarity decide to surface.

And now, while driving in the countryside on the way to give a meditation teaching session in a small town, I gaze out the car window and onto a wheat field, where many scarecrows are all standing in a group next to each other. With curiosity, I stop at the side of the road and observe the spectacle before me. The scarecrows are clad in a variety of colourful clothing. After a few more moments of observation, I realise that one is dressed as Elvis Presley and another as Santa Claus. The radical creativity that has manifested itself to form this congregation of some twenty-five scarecrows gives rise to a new level of Presence within me.

There are no birds within eyesight of this area and it seems almost silent as I walk towards the field of wheat. I navigate the circumference of the artistic grouping and feel vibes of amusement wash through my body. Ominous are some of the scarecrows, as I look up at them staring down on me.

I spend a couple more minutes pondering the detail in the individual costumes and dresses that make up these fascinating creations. Okay, it's time to get back on the road and cherish this bizarre experience for what it is.

And now, I arrive at the petrol station in the darkness of night to witness thousands of Christmas beetles swarming around the lights. This is something I have never experienced before. A strong sense of Presence arises and when I open the car door, a deafening sound of buzzing and humming escalates as I realise nature has forced this species of insect into a restricted space.

While filling up the tank, I am present to hundreds of squashed dead golden-coloured beetles on the ground where previous car wheels would have driven on exit from the station. My mind is intervening and asking, *Why? Why? Why?* So, I go to pay for the petrol and ask the attendant if this bug invasion has occurred previously. The attendant said that the smoke from the bush burning on the nearby hill forced thousands of beetles to flee and, during their journey, they were attracted to stop at the service station lights.

Amazed, I return to the car and spend a minute reflecting on the behaviour of nature and feeling the abundant energy and vibration generated by a mass of shiny hard-shelled beetles. I drive away, glancing in the rear view mirror to capture an image of a surreal and unique experience.

And now, from a twelfth floor office balcony, a New Year's Eve fireworks show heralds in another calendar year full of possibilities. The continued explosion of thunderous sound followed by showers of colour and shapes decorating the night sky escalates Presence in the most wondrous ways.

A tingling sensation travels up the middle of my back and up through the crown of my head. Feelings of ecstasy pour out the top of my head like a fountain and light up the night sky in its own figurative way. I see this as my physical form recycling the universe's energy and putting it back out there.

Whilst in the midst of this festive experience of saying goodbye to 'the old' and welcoming in 'the new', my mind begs the question, *How can they create fireworks that make smiley faces and love hearts, bizarre whistling sounds and several staggered layers of smaller light and colour explosions within the one big firework?* So, standing and watching the continual bonanza without placing any labels or analysis on the event, Presence rises again to a whole new level. The wonderment on people's faces next to me is inspirational. There is an overwhelming collective sense of joy here right now.

And now, physically exhausted in bed, trying to go to sleep, I am present to a soft, deep humming noise of some sort. It is keeping me awake, and yet I do not have the energy to get up and investigate its origin and do something to silence it. So instead, it becomes the background for a mantra phrase, "Ah Hum", which I start repeating to myself. And eventually I fall asleep.

Now, awake again in the middle of the night to the same sound, my mind becomes more disturbed. Rolling out of bed and planting my feet slowly and firmly on the floor, I proceed to allow consciousness to guide me to wherever the noise is originating from. In near pitch-black, I start walking towards the window. The sound is getting louder. My hand reaches up to slide shut the slightly ajar window. And now there is complete silence. Without putting too much thought into the solved situation, I realise a vacuum of airflow was being choked between the roof air-conditioned vent and the window across the other side of the bedroom.

Back in bed now, and the sound of silence is causing a mild ringing noise in my ears. So, bringing the breath to centre stage, I allow its soft sound and gentle current to lull me into a state of sleep once again.

And now, looking up at the stars in wonderment of the universe's vastness, I observe in awe the many clusters of bright twinkly lights. The longer I look in stillness, the more lights, shapes and shades appear. There is absolute silence. Out of the corner of my eye, I see a moving light among the stars. With concentration and an air of excitement, I fix my gaze on it and follow it as it traverses across the dark night sky.

The mind starts asking what it is. *Is it a plane? A meteor? A shooting star that I should quickly make a wish on? Where did it come from? How come I did not see it earlier? How fast is it travelling?* I take a few deep breaths and intentionally muffle the inquiring voices in my head to simply enjoy this fleeting moment in time.

Quickly the moving light disappears somewhere into the distance. I spend the next few moments reflecting on what I cannot explain and the power, energy and beauty associated with what was just witnessed. Beyond any words, the universe never ceases to amaze me. It is challenging sometimes to fathom that we as human beings originated from stardust.

And now, I move my body joyfully from side to side, humming to the harmonics of Stevie Wonder's song, 'Isn't She Lovely'. With headphones wrapped around my ears, all other noises are cancelled out as I watch Stevie perform live at a tribute to Nelson Mandela on my iPhone.

I feel his limbic resonance that translates out to thousands of people, dominated by his abundance of happiness and love. His music permeates my soul. My mind intervenes with the question: *I wonder how Stevie can maintain such a deep sense of joy when he is blind?*

"Pure bliss and enlightenment is not necessarily associated with the functions of all five senses," comes the answer that arises out of consciousness. I suddenly feel the Presence of spirit among many people, animals and nature in Divine Consciousness as I continue to swoon along to this fabulous soul-massaging song.

Now, the music begins to fade and the song comes to an end before a moment of silence followed by a large eruption of jubilation from the audience in recognition of harmony. I rest in awareness and Being for a few moments and feel a deep sense of serenity and peace.

Mindlessness

Being closed minded and not open to many possibilities used to be a normal part of everyday life for me. Subconsciously I was too frightened to wonder about anything out of the ordinary in fear I was not going to be comfortable with the discovery. Also I used to think that if I asked questions about something that was curious in nature, then the answer may appear too obvious and I would face scrutiny and ridicule for not knowing it in the first place. Wondering seemed to me to be a waste of time; a type of daydreaming.

Techniques to Apply

Inquire further about something until you are satisfied with the answer. Find something that you have never thought of before that is totally unfamiliar to you, research it briefly and journal your findings. Next time you are amongst nature, approach something new with heightened curiosity and be inquisitive.

CHAPTER 16

MEDITATING & AWAKENING

How Mindfulness Helps

T he more you meditate, the easier it is to practice being mindful. And the more mindful you are, the probability of being awakened increases. It becomes a deeply peaceful and pleasant cycle.

Mindfulness in turn makes it easier to meditate. You end up making time to sit in silence, reflect and contemplate the present moment without effort. You also understand that meditation does not only constitute sitting cross-legged in the lotus position with a straight back, eyes closed and hands open. You acknowledge that meditation can be performed with eyes open whilst walking. A mindful lifestyle knows that life is a journey and not a destination.

The Diary

And now, standing naked in front of the mirror and simply observing the human body that God gave me, gives rise to the question, *Who Am I?* After some time of continually staring at myself, the mind asks, *Who Is That?* More moments go by analysing the colour, shapes and contours of my body parts before a shift occurs right here in perfect stillness. The conscious observer of the mind and physical body is present.

There are no words that can really describe this moment. What I do know is that I am accepting of who I Am. Now, feelings of gratitude, love, joy and peace engulf my Being. Wonderful sensations and feelings overwhelm me as I gradually raise both corners of my mouth to produce a smile.

After a few more minutes, the mind re-enters the present moment and starts sending signals to my feet that is time to move on physically. And because I refuse to move just now, in this next moment, the mind sends signals to my stomach, alerting it to go eat food. This is amusing because not only have I just eaten breakfast, but the mind is becoming bored and restless in this foreign territory of nude stillness, doing everything it can to lure me away from this full-length mirror. I know exactly what is happening here.

And now, I am awoken suddenly by a loud and distinct KNOCK, KNOCK, KNOCK sound. It appears to be originating from outside the bedroom door. In a semi-conscious state, I swing my legs out of bed and walk towards the en suite, wondering what the noise is. Quickly realising it is not an intruder or prankster, I go to the toilet before settling back down in between the crisp warm sheets to drift back into a dreamlike state.

Still feeling apprehensive, I attempt to close my eyes on a number of occasions without success. Tingling sensations vibrate throughout my physical body, originating in the heart. From the inside out, I continue to feel more vibrations coming in waves, growing stronger.

In the absence of light at 3am, my first instinct is to resist the sensations by sitting upright in bed; however a deeper level of consciousness gives me a level of comfort that this experience is natural and to be enjoyed. So I surrender to the Isness of this experience and allow whatever is occurring to continue.

Engulfed in pure bliss now, I feel as if I am being physically lifted above the mattress. When I try to slide my hand between my back and bed to see if I am indeed levitating, I soon realise gravity is playing its part by keeping me attached to the bed. Overwhelming feelings of deep love run through my veins. My pulse rate is slower than normal and I am not sweating. As each moment unfolds, I feel intense gratitude for this incredible encounter. I drift off to sleep.

Awakened at dawn by birds singing a call and response duet, I regain consciousness and get up out of bed to open the curtains. As I start walking, I feel so much lighter – as if I've lost 5 kilos of body weight. A quick check in the bathroom mirror and measure standing on the scales reveals that I am still the same 75 kilos I was yesterday. What happened?

And now, I have found my way into a discussion about the belief in heaven and hell. One person comments that Jesus was God on earth and he was placed here over two thousand years ago to save us. In a non-judgemental way, I acknowledge this view. And without thought, I offer the view that God consciousness already exists in human beings and that when people quiet their chattering minds for long enough, the Presence of God begins to rise from within our inner space.

As I am communicating this belief to the people involved in this conversation, I begin to feel comfortably overwhelmed with bliss, peace, joy, compassion and abundant love. And in an ecstatic state of Being, a few tears start rolling down my cheeks. There is now another shift in consciousness occurring within me as I am enlightened to the belief that heaven and God lives within me here, there and everywhere around.

What an incredible relief it is to know that as human beings we do not have to wait until we return our bodies to the earth for the soul to go to heaven when it is right here, right now.

And now, I wake up in the middle of the night with the fascinating experience of being highly alert and aware of the real me – Consciousness re-entering my physical body. It is amazing to reflect on the descending that occurs back into the body before becoming conscious and the eyes opening.

An analogy to describe this situation could be like the landing of an aircraft on the runway. Gradually the airborne spirit travels down, getting closer and closer until touch down. It was so vivid and noticeable. The touchdown of consciousness back into my physical body was smooth. I could see my body on the bed curled up and became excited as I got closer to physical re-entry. In this moment I became awakened to the fact that I am pure consciousness inhabiting this human body.

Now I am smiling in wonderment and awe at an awakening experience of a new kind. And now, after a couple of minutes of reflection, my mind utters to me: *Can you imagine if that had been a rough landing? You would have been sweating and gasping for breath!* I witness the thought with a degree of amusement, close my eyes and go back to sleep.

And now, as I gently close my eyes and settle into the breath, the rising and falling of the chest and abdomen is ever present. As I take the next inhale, I observe the air entering my left nostril is more free-flowing than the air entering the passage of my right nostril. Continuing to ride the waves of the life force for a few more minutes, I am overcome by a deeper sense of calm and relaxation.

A thought bubbles up to the surface; I simply witness it in a nonjudgmental way, resisting an urge to scratch it and focus on the next breath instead.

As I take a step up into consciousness, I again pose the question, *Who Am I?* No answer is forthcoming, so I continue to rest in awareness. The inquiry continues with, *How can I best be of service?* Again nothing comes to mind.

My chattering mind is now curious as to what is going on. The next inhale and exhale softly closes the door on its inquisitive form. I then ask myself, *What is my purpose?* And completely let go.

Having faith that the universe will indeed at some point in time respond with an answer, I take another step into consciousness. My pulse rate is slower and less forceful. The space between each shallower breath lengthens.

What am I grateful for? Ask and I will receive, knowing that the answers already exist. I await patiently as they will eventually reveal themselves.

Silently I start repeating *I am, I am, I am* and begin to drop further into awareness above the canvas of my mind. It is peaceful here right now. Outside the dimension of time, I simply rest in Being.

A blue pulsating light presents itself in the middle of my eyebrow centre. With eyes still closed, I acknowledge its beauty and marvel at the theta waves being released by my brain.

And now, for something completely different, I am sitting in a steam room being very still and settling into my breath. With my eyes slightly open, I have a soft gaze present to the thick, heated mist that causes the skin to cry with beads of sweat.

My circumstances are a true testament that meditation can be done anywhere, anyhow, anytime for as long or as little as you like. The mind makes the comment, *Gee, it's getting hot in here,* and starts to build a story around why steam rooms can be good and bad for my health.

In this moment I pay attention to the drops of clear, salty liquid falling from my eyebrows and trickling down my legs, arms and stomach. Observing the glistening light decorating the tops of each bead of sweat buys me a longer gap between thoughts.

Feeling a real sense of Presence and Consciousness, I no longer notice the hot temperature in the steam room and continue to rest in awareness for a longer period.

Now stepping out of the steam room and into a cold shower gives birth immediately to a new sense of Presence filled with vitality and alertness. I gasp for breath as the chilled water cascades down my spine.

And now, sitting quietly and still on a wooden bench in a church's meditation garden, there is a strong sense of serenity and Presence. The Swedish Christmas mass service that just finished set the scene for contemplation on the birth of one of the most enlightened beings to ever walk this earth: Jesus Christ.

The late afternoon heralds a choir of cicadas singing in unison whilst a cool breeze comes and goes. Gradually a ray of sunlight breaks through a cloud and beams onto the bench where I sit. The warmth of the sun is soothing on the skin of my hands. Butterflies floating past are suddenly whisked away by the wind.

It feels so calm and peaceful to simply look and listen. A pinecone falls off a giant overhanging tree and just misses my head. There is such a beautiful conscious energy present and I start to sense the spirits of others around. After about half an hour and having transcended into a state of bliss, a few tears of joy roll down my cheeks.

And now, I am present whilst sitting comfortably in a cane chair on the back deck of my brother's house after a hearty Christmas Day lunch. A storm starts to build as others join me for a practice in Presence. It is taking a few minutes for the chattering mind still engaged in past conversation with several relatives to subside. As the gaps begin to widen in between thoughts, I become aware of water trickling down the tiled roof next door caused by the gentle drops of rain falling from the sky. Four other family members sit next to me and start mimicking what I am doing – which is simply none other than being still, looking and listening to the natural surroundings of plants and water.

There is a big clap of thunder as the sky darkens and soon the rain becomes so forceful, it appears as several water poles attached from the sky down to the grassed earth. The energy is causing a new vibration in the air and I become alert again to a waterfall of H2O cascading down the surrounding roofs. Loved ones sitting next to me are smiling in awe of nature's power. I sense the family unity of collective consciousness in this moment.

The landscape has changed considerably in less than an hour now, as the storm begins to subside. New puddles of water glisten under the moonlight, droplets decorate thousands of leaf tips, and the high-pitched sound of silence is ringing. A fresh sense of cleansing Presence moves through every cell in my physical body. Nostrils flare as deeper breaths are drawn in to absorb the re-energised sweet smells of nature. Eyes widen to view the brighter green colours of plants.

And now, one bird chirps, breaking the silence, before several other feathered creatures join the harmonious choir.

And now, it is dark and silent as I sit on the toilet seat inside a tiny restroom cubicle, connecting with my breath. On this frantically busy day, this is the only way I can get a few minutes for a meditation practice. As I repeat to myself the self-made mantra, *health, wealth, joy*, eventually the warm tranquillity of transcendence transpires.

I drop into the vastness of inner space. Wow, it is so wonderful! In this present moment, there is no connection with human form and purely an identification with the real me – pure consciousness; Presence of the formless. I am here, there and everywhere. Floating in outer space with no gravity could be a way to describe the current experience, yet I am physically located in between four walls and a roof no wider than one metre and no longer than two metres.

In between my eyebrow centre appears a beautiful pulsating blue light with no defined shape. It comes and goes periodically. Resting here in Being can no longer be described in words. Eventually I open my eyes and feel rebooted and refreshed to face the next phase of this physical form world.

And now, sitting on the edge of a sandbank at the beach, being still and quiet whilst viewing and listening to both the form world and the subtle formless world, I rediscover again that I am pure consciousness observing my physical body. There is something magical about being amongst the vastness of wide expanses of the sand and where the horizon meets the ocean line. The rhythmic and deliberate sounds of crashing waves, the salty taste and smell of the ocean air and the feel of the earth pulsing below my feet become all so mesmerising.

After fixing a soft gaze on a distant island for a while, a transformation takes place as I make my way over there in spirit and leave my form body sitting in the sand. Minutes later, a flock of seagulls lands right in front of my legs. They seem curious. There is no food to offer them and the next gust of wind sweeps them off the sand and they fly away gracefully.

Glancing at my watch indicates that I have been here in meditation for over ninety minutes.

In the distance, I hear the faint voice of my son asking what is being cooked for dinner because everyone is hungry. Smiling in peace and love, I get up and mindfully observe each barefoot step taken on the sand whilst feeling the sensation of a micro foot massage under the soles on the way back to the cabin.

Mindlessness

Once upon a time I thought meditation was for cult followers of the Hare Krishna kind and that you had to wear an orange gown with a shaved head to participate. I would ridicule anyone I saw sitting with legs crossed and eyes closed in stillness. And my definition of awakening used to be when your best friend poured a glass of cold water on you because you were too drunk to wake up the next morning.

I was too busy criticising those participating in this ancient practice to better their lives on the path to enlightenment, and in the meantime suffered for being mindless and judgmental without even knowing it myself.

Techniques to Apply

Put this book down right now and sit in stillness and silence for three minutes with eyes closed (or open), whilst paying full attention to each inhale and exhale of the breath. Surrender to the universe, set an intention, ask and let go.

Write down three things that *Now & Now* has awakened you to.

CHAPTER 17

THEIR HEALING

And now, after overcoming a major life challenge and experiencing an incredible awakening, Deidre recounts her magical experience in the present moment of Being on the beach surrounded by the ocean on two occasions.

"My soul absorbs the wisdom of the full moon, gently inviting me to create space for earthly healing and compassion, focusing on inner peace and balance. My naked body drinks from the glow of the full moon that spreads out across the roaring swollen ocean. My entire being is reflected in the warm, salty water, the thrashing waves cleansing my soul, opening my heart and invigorating my body. Under this full moon, I am the woman who owns herself and is whole unto herself. And from our relationship, I am learning that I am whole unto myself, able to take in new experiences and be changed by them.

"And now, as I walk along the beach this afternoon, I feel the wind move around my body in ways I have never felt before. It is like a lover gently caressing my skin with his lips, his hot breath making my hair stand on end. It is such a subtle whisper of breath over my body at first; then, as the wind picks up, it is like he is ravishing my body with his desperate lips, his breath getting heavier and labouring with desire. It is so intense it takes my breath away, and in this moment, I realise what it truly means to be in love with life, because it is in love with me and I am life!"

And now, after many years since first experiencing a traumatic event in a peace keeping mission during a life-or-death situation, Todd narrates his current day experience in a state of mindfulness.

"I can sense in advance when the memories of being in the Presence of five dead colleagues at the morgue is about to arise. It has been over twenty years since the event. In this moment, I start taking a few deeper breaths in and out and become aware of my body. As the thought arises, I acknowledge this is now only a voice in my head and the past does not exist anymore. The thought lingers and tries to seduce me into depression, however I simply refocus on the next breath and continue paying attention to the smell and taste of this sip of coffee. The thought dissolves and I smile whilst acknowledging the vagueness and shortness of the memory that once plagued and paralysed my Being.

"I know now that I am consciousness, able to observe my thoughts and not identify with them. This is making a huge difference in a positive way to how the body responds to dramatic events of the past and worries about my future. It is a long road to healing but I am at peace with life and understand that a regular mindfulness practice and maintenance program is helping me to cope with Post-Traumatic Stress Disorder."

And now, Josephine reflects on the fact that she no longer suffers after years of severe migraines due to her growing practice of meditation and yoga exercises.

"It continues to amaze me that I am pain free from severe headaches without any medication and by purely paying attention to my body whilst stilling the chattering mind previously so worried about what needed to be done next. In this present moment as I move my body on the mat, being attentive to each subtle movement, I exhale any negativity and inhale a new outlook. There is a release of internal blockages in my neck, spine, shoulders and back with each gentle stretch. Tension disappears instantaneously as I feel more and think less.

"The breath is so powerful that it has been able to subconsciously offset any suffering as a result of migraines that were previously debilitating. The pain body is almost non-existent now. Something has happened in my brain that mystifies me and it is fabulous. And at a deeper level, the transformation is occurring with what cannot be explained logically other than a protection from the subtle world I cannot see with my eyes, but I can feel it all around and in my head. Wow, what a wonderful, free anaesthetic wave riding on breaths is, simultaneously resting in the gap between nonsense thinking!"

And now, Greg has a breakthrough with his meditation practice and finally experiences those long gaps of pure consciousness in between what used to be a very overactive mind. He also reveals a bonus revelation.

"So at the moment I feel at peace more than ever before. A sense of tranquillity engulfs my Being, regardless of the household chaos that is occurring right now with the demands of two very young children. I am observing a mind that is continually trying to intervene and ring alarm bells in my head about this current situation. There is no need to jump up in a panic and clean that spilled juice over there, or tell Issie to stop singing out loud because it is annoying her younger brother.

"This next breath is full of gratitude for two happy children who bring so much joy into the world and my life. Every second spent with them is a blessing and since I have been able to get out of my head and into my heart, the flow of collective consciousness with the family is nothing less than blissful.

"It is nothing less than delightful to sit back and observe these little munchkins totally uninhibited and live through their inquisitive eyes. I am also part of them and they are part of me. Together we are growing."

And now, Kevin journals how he mindfully takes care of his damaged knee moment by moment during a yoga class. The doctor told him he would never run again after the operation. Lucky he listened to his intuition and not the doctor, because he is running again thanks to yoga and mindfulness practices.

"As I come into Tree Pose, Half Pigeon and Airplane in this heated yoga room, attention is paid to the muscles, tendons and ligaments surrounding the joint of my healing knee. With each movement I breathe reenergising vibes into the area and soften into the yoga pose gently. I am confident I will be able to heal the knee with the combination of strengthening movements, focused attention and trust in the force of the universe. Jogging is fine now, as long as I follow up straight away with a few yoga stretches.

"When changing the angle of the affected knee, I pay acute attention to how it feels every second and know the boundaries that I must stay within. It is a lesson for me to let go of the ego and not push myself or compare to other people, and not to succumb to the tempting voice in the head.

"In meditation now, I repeat the mantra: *I am healthy, I am*. As I repeat the mantra, I feel a warm and ticklish sensation in my damaged knee. The mind is powerful. It can direct healing energy into areas of my body."

And now, Joe talks about his transformation from years of regularly losing his temper to being calm and peaceful in the same situations.

"Now, when sensations and feelings arise in my body associated with anger, I acknowledge the increase in heartbeat, the hair at the back of my neck rising and the queasiness in my stomach. Before they get too strong and take control, I observe and understand that this is just the mind trying to seduce me into misery. The breath has become my ever-reliable anchor and friend to dissolve a potentially nasty situation. So I take as little as one deep inhale through my nose and count to five, then pause for one second before counting down from five to one on the exhale. It is amazing as it works every time!

"It never ceases to amaze that the breath is free, better than drugs, no side effects and can be done anywhere and anytime for as long or as little time as may be available.

"I still wonder every now and then why I had not found out about this mindfulness practice earlier in life. If only I had known, maybe I would not have caused so much pain and destruction."

And now, Julie, a happy-go-lucky person with no challenging situations to report on, describes a moment of pure bliss from her continued search for a deeper joy within.

"Right now I am feeling so loved, but not by anyone in particular. It is like I have the arms of God wrapped around me and through me. It feels really peaceful and I cannot stop smiling. A few tears of joy trickle down my cheeks as I cherish being in this moment so very much.

"A few great ideas for a design project I am working on appear in my tranquil mind. It is fascinating and somewhat ironic because I was not even deliberately thinking of any ideas. Sitting here with a blank stare looking out onto a field of green grass, the ideas surfaced like bubbles of air from under the water.

"I knew I'd always been a jolly person, but I was always curious whether there was something deeper than happiness in many moments. I discovered by continuing to fine-tune my attention to being present, talking less and listening more, that a deep sense of joy washes over and through my Being.

"I am in awe at the way the universe works, people are born and develop, and nature organises itself. I wonder about the subtle world that cannot be seen with the naked eye. It never ceases to amaze me that the majority of society can function day to day without the same awareness I have about the meaning of life."

And now, Stu tells of overcoming the Obsessive Compulsive Disorder that restricted his life and employment opportunities for so many years.

"As I go about washing my hands, it is tempting to pick up the bar of soap fifty times and swipe it between each finger three times before rinsing off with water and drying them for two minutes. Instead I recognise that my mind is trying again to make me return to old behavioural patterns. By focusing on the visual surroundings in the bathroom and the sound of my breath plus the smell of the soap, I am able to move forward by only touching the bar of soap once, rinsing my hands in a few seconds and drying them in less than thirty seconds. My next phase in recovery from OCD is to stop counting all together and labelling timeframes. It is a work in progress and, thanks to a mindfulness practice, I am feeling more accepted by society than ever before.

"I don't know the details of neuroplasticity but I trust that by changing habits and being diligent with daily meditation over the last year, I am not reacting in the same obsessive ways as in the past. All I know is that a meditation and mindfulness practice has changed my life for the better. People do not avoid me so much anymore and instead are happy to converse with me more often."

And now, Maria shares a Present Moment Living experience that previously haunted her with the memory of being violently abused as a child. She is now able to acknowledge that the past does not exist anymore and the pain body associated with her Past Traumatic Stress has been dissolved.

"Right now, I am in a kids' park, watching my children play on the swings, slipping down the slide and jumping off the wooden fort. A child screams in pain as she slips, trips over and falls on her face. I am suddenly reminded of when my mother used to repeatedly hit me hard on my head with her shoe until I started bleeding.

"The breathing is my anchor and I immediately connect with each inhale and exhale while forcing a prolonged smile. I am separated from the voices in my head and previous memories. The flashback of when I was a child dissolves instantly and does not surface again. I attempt to help the fallen child but the mother runs over before I can get there. She yells at her child for not being careful when playing.

"I step back and continue to focus on my breathing, paying attention to one footstep at a time as I quietly return to the park bench. The wind cools my face and I look up at the tree branches swaying. I feel grateful for being alive and having wonderful children whom I love and do not harm in any way."

Mindlessness

Living in the past and identifying with it, worrying about the future and being closed to new beginnings are all symptoms of a mindlessness practice. A lack of gratitude for life and unwillingness to break old habits can limit the process of healing required to move forward and not backwards.

Techniques to Apply

The next time you are confronted with a challenging situation, take a few minutes to document how you mindfully dealt with the situation. Reflect in silence on the transformation you have begun to experience. Make a mindfulness practice a part of your life.

Be open to art of the possible.

EPILOGUE

So now, the mindfulness journey continues. Having come from a place of torment, frustration, anger, stress and a concern for what others thought about me (just to name a few mindless terms), I find myself at this moment in a state of deep contentment regardless of circumstances. This is best described by a recent word I saw on my brother's Facebook page:

> *"Unfuckwithable" – adj. When you are truly at peace and in touch with yourself, nothing anyone says or does bothers you and no negativity can touch you. Also see: chillaxed, zenstate, unfadeable, innerpeace, canttouchthis.*

During my transformation of present moment living, I have produced an eleven-track guided mindfulness meditation audio album, *Renew U*, and written three other books (soon to be published):

1) A simple handbook to help those suffering from Post-Traumatic Stress Disorder and their loved ones and carers
2) A fun children's mindfulness book of poems
3) A reference guide to growing younger

Please keep an eye out for the release of these books at either robginnivan.com or various bookstores and online shops.

As I travel down and up the path of an evolving life, living in the present moment, more and more people in society are coming into view having also adapted a mindfulness practice. There is no doubt you know people who could benefit from this 'new way of being', so I encourage you to buy them a copy of this book or lend them yours. Change habits, feel better, live longer and be in the Now.

Printed in the United States
By Bookmasters